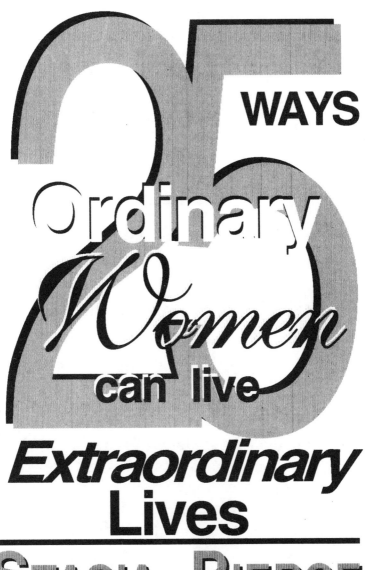

25 WAYS

Ordinary *Women* can live

Extraordinary Lives

STACIA PIERCE

1st Printing

*25 Ways Ordinary Women Can Live
Extraordinary Lives*

ISBN: 1-886-880-23-9
Copyright © 1999 by Stacia Pierce
Published by Life Changers Publishing
808 Lake Lansing Rd. Ste. 200
East Lansing, MI 48823

TABLE OF CONTENTS

PART I LEARN

PART II: LOVE

PART III: LAUGH

DEDICATION

TO MY HUSBAND JAMES PIERCE;
WHO CELEBRATES MY CAUSE.

Acknowledgements

I Sincerely Appreciate many of my friends and family members whose contributions I acknowledge with great joy.

Ryan and Ariana who give me so many extraordinary ideas.

Alfred and Phyllis Scott my parents, and Rosalind Threatt my sister, all of whom keep encouraging me to write books.

Tracy Forbes and Frances Brown, my loyal, long-time friends who celebrate my every endeavor.

Renee Hornbuckle and Adriane Wilson my very generous and supportive friends.

Sharlette Marshall, my creativity partner.

Ruth Reed, Sabrina Todd and Niki Woolfolk, my editorial team.

The Women's Leadership Team and all of the ladies of LCCC who support every single project I take on.

INTRODUCTION

To Live an Extraordinary life, every woman
must know how:

TO LEARN

TO LOVE

TO LAUGH...

PART I: LEARN

 Dare To Dream

"Extraordinary dreams come true when ordinary people have an extraordinary amount of determination."
-Walt Kallestad

What is a dream? It's your creative vision of your future. It's what you want your life to become. A friend of mine heard me speak at a women's conference on the subject and she told me it was like a light bulb went off in her head. She said that for so long she was afraid to dream and to want big things, but once she heard me talk about dreaming, she realized that it doesn't cost anything to dream. It's true; dreaming doesn't cost you anything, well, except a little bit of time. But to fulfill your dream will cost you determination.

There is no right or wrong formula for how you should dream. The key is to dream big, keep it simple, start where you are, and work on reaching your dreams each day. I like how Peter Daniels describes dreaming. He says, "In dreaming you are creating something out of nothing. In so doing you position yourself on the periphery of God likeness.

13

You become a mini creature without substance or form, you create an image of an idea or event you intend to pursue and it will take a tangible shape."[1] I can remember when I dared to dream about writing my very first book, "Beauty the Inside Story." I was such a novice at the time. I had no real knowledge or prior experience about book writing, but I had an idea and a story to tell. Determined, I plunged into the project with the help of friends. As a result, my dream was fulfilled when the book was completed. I can remember receiving the first shipment of my book. It was awesome to me- opening that box and seeing my words in print. There was such a sense of accomplishment.

After a while I realized that if I was going to continue writing books, I needed to learn more about how to write. I needed to take some courses on writing. I began journalizing so that I could develop my own writing style. I also needed an audience who wanted to buy my books. It was time for me to do some research to better fulfill my dream of being an author. I went on to write eleven leadership manuals, and several books, became editor-in-chief of my own, W.O.R.D. magazine, was chosen to be on the advisory board of some major magazines and the dream is still unfolding. This year I have three new books that were released simultaneously. As you can see, my dream didn't happen overnight. It took hard work and applying specific principles to fulfill them. Here are the keys that worked for me and that can help you live out your dream.

Write Your Dream Down

Your dreams cannot take root unless they are written. Writing your dream down will help you begin to focus on making those dreams a reality. The more information you put on paper the greater probability that you will succeed. Have you gotten so comfortable with your life that you have forgotten to dream? God has exciting plans and a bright future laid out for you, but you must grasp it by faith. Writing down your dreams is putting your faith into action.

Ever since I began to write my dreams down in my Prayer & Purpose Planner, I have seen God orchestrate my life in such a way that just about every dream I desired has been realized. My dream list is long and intricate. Some of my dreams may take a lifetime to fulfill but just looking forward to the dreams being fulfilled make the journey so rewarding.

Have a Dream Day

Schedule a monthly dream day where you get by yourself and take the time to review and reflect on your dreams. During your dream day update your dreams by adding inspiring pictures to them. Then spend time meditating on your dream. I always begin my dream day with prayer and tuning in to the Holy Spirit. I record what God is saying about my dreams. Many times God gives me instructions that will cause my dreams to manifest much quicker than me trying to accomplish them on my own.

Oftentimes, women feel like their life is too insignificant to dream big, so they settle for living an average lifestyle. You are very significant to God, He created you to solve a problem for someone. People are counting on you to dream big. **So Start dreaming like a kid again;** stretch your mind to envision doing what you really love as if there were no limitations. When you dream, you stretch your vision and standards, gain direction and attract your dream towards you like a magnet.

Pray Over Your Dreams

When you dream big, commit your dreams to God through prayer. God will go to work on your behalf to make your dreams come to pass. In my life I have seen God work miraculously on my behalf to cause my dreams to manifest. Did you know that most of your dreams are seeds that God has planted in your heart? Jerry Sevelle said, "Once God has planted a dream within your heart, He has every intention of bringing it to pass. I Thessalonians 5:24 says, "Faithful is He who called you and He also will bring it to pass."

Prepare For Your Dreams

One important step in your daring to dream process is properly preparing for the dream. The biggest mistake you can make is to step out to accomplish a dream unprepared. What do you need to successfully fulfill your dream? It could be increased knowledge about your area of interest or a better vocabulary so you can communicate your dreams to everyone. You may need mentors who will encourage you and help show you the way or some physical adjustments so you are properly equipped to fit your dream's description.

17

In your journal, write about your dreams. Express your feelings about what you want and how you will go about achieving it. Also, journalize about where you're really at in life. I can remember journalizing about one of my dreams and I came to the conclusion that I needed more insight, wisdom and knowledge before I stepped out in that area. So I waited until I was fully equipped, then I proceeded and when I accomplished that dream it was a smashing success. Be in more of a hurry to prepare for your dream than to accomplish your dream.

I once knew of a lady who, after seeing my women's ministry, decided to begin an international women's ministry for Pastors's wives and women in leadership. She heard me briefly talk about doing something similar to this and decided to jump on it. She wasn't familiar with ministering to women and had no experience ministering to leaders. Needless to say, her idea failed. This was a classic case of stepping out unprepared. When your dream is big, you have to prepare big. **Don't change direction without first an inspection.** If she would have investigated, she would have seen that I have poured years of ministry into my own women at our church, which was my proving and training ground. I travel often to do some sort of women's conference or leadership training. All of our outreach ministries have grown fairly large at our church. We have fellowship groups for Men, Women, Singles and Married Couples and I was responsible for training all of those leaders to run their groups. Therefore, when I mentioned stepping out and possibly helping pastor's wives and women in leadership one day, I had already had some experience in how to set up and grow a ministry. Proper preparation always precedes lasting success. Begin today to make a daily investment in upgrading your knowledge, skills and wisdom so you can soon realize your dreams.

Create a V.I.P. Dream List

Who you are connected to is going to play an important part in your dreams coming to pass. Successful people can provide a wealth of information and insight to help you achieve your dreams much quicker.

Think of the people you admire; what is it about them that you like? Have you ever wanted to meet a famous author? A movie star? A prominent speaker or minister?

What about the president? Studies have shown that you are only six people away from anyone in the world you want to meet. The entire world is open to you. You can meet just about anyone you really want to meet, but you have to start with writing a dream list of people you want to meet. When you write it down you make the vision more tangible. Then write down three questions you would ask them if you met them. My husband James applied this principle. While traveling last year, flying from New York to Detroit he had the privilege of being on the plane with Muhamad and meeting him. While in New York on a shopping trip I got on the same elevator as Joan Rivers, who was shopping with her dog in tote.

I'm always ready for a divine connection. You never know when they will emerge. Once you create a V.I. P. dream list you'll began to meet important people who aren't on your list, but are valuable to accomplishing your destiny. **Never enter the presence of greatness without recognition.** This is a valuable principle that will take you far in life. Too many times we shy away from recognition because of jealousy or timidity operating in us. Anyone who has a level of greatness has paid a tremendous price for it. When we recognize greatness, we are then able to glean from the wisdom and experience encompassed in that person.

20

Only Participate in Dream Building
Relationships

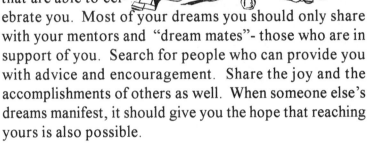

Let's face it; there will be those that celebrate you and those that do not. Share your dream with those people that are able to celebrate you. Most of your dreams you should only share with your mentors and "dream mates"- those who are in support of you. Search for people who can provide you with advice and encouragement. Share the joy and the accomplishments of others as well. When someone else's dreams manifest, it should give you the hope that reaching yours is also possible.

The most miserable and jealous people in life are those who have lost hope in their dreams or have no dreams at all. When my book, *25 Ways Women Can Motivate Themselves*, began to do really well in the bookstores, and we began to receive daily inquiries for speaking engagements, I mentioned the status of this project to an associate of mine. Immediately they began to compare my book with another well-known author who has sold millions of copies. I could recognize the jealousy. Instead of saying, "I'm proud of you" or "how exciting," they instantly tried to deflate the significance of what was taking place in my life. If that has happened to you, chalk it up as insight and don't share your success stories with that person again. I refuse to hang around people who don't celebrate my dreams or who claim they don't care about having dreams, because eventually they will try to pull you down to their boring, mundane lifestyle.

Step Out on Your Dreams Despite the Critics

You must be ready to face the consequences of stepping out and doing your dreams. When you step out, you will inspire some and make critics of others. When I first started women's ministry I sought God and created my own unique style of ministry. Most of the people I knew thought what I was doing was insignificant to the church body, but now, my dream has outgrown me. Women all over the country are now inspired to do women's ministry. Many have inquired of me concerning set up and maintaining a women's ministry. When you begin living out your dream, you will be an encouragement to others to live out their dreams.

From now on, give a lot of thought to your dreams and your future, because that's where you will spend the rest of your life. Don't ever lose your dreams! Even if it looks like they are never going to come to pass. Dreams are what give you motivation in life, a reason for existence.

22

You may feel like your dream is insignificant, and that it won't make a difference if you pursue it or not. However, remember that every God given dream has an impact beyond it's size. Dare to dream today!

Dream Tips Summary

1. Set aside five minutes everyday to pray about your dreams.

2. Visualize your dreams coming to pass. Use your Prayer & Purpose Planner to add faith photos to your dreams.

3. Pray for your dream building relationships-relationships that are healthy, spark creativity, inspire innovation, and cause you to be more productive.

4. Find a mentor who shares your core values and gives you insight and information.

5. Develop your skills and talent so you can be successful at living out your dream.

6. Categorize your dreams as such: family, children, marriage, career, spiritual, travel and personal development.

7. Set a dream date to review, pray and plan how you will reach your dreams.

8. Visit places that will inspire your imagination- places that will stimulate you to continue dreaming.

9. Start working on your dreams by first working on yourself.

10. Read the book, *Mental Toughness for Success*, by Dr. Ira Hilliard. To order call: 218-875-4448

Idea File:

I agree with T.E. Lawrence who said: "*All men dream, but not equally. Those who dream by night in the daily recesses of their minds wake in the day to find it was vanity; but the dreamers of the day are dangerous men (or women) for they may bet on their dreams with open eyes to make it possible.*"

Now you are ready to dare to dream yourself. Take a few minutes and write down your dreams. What are some of your dreams in life? Do you dream of better health, more money, a fulfilling career, a bigger house, an ideal vacation, a luxury car, a new wardrobe, global travel, more friends, financial independence, more time for yourself and family or becoming more spiritual? Go ahead and write a list of twenty dreams.

My Dream List

1.

2.

3.

4.

5.

6.

7.

8.

9.

10.

11.

12.

13..

14.

15.

16.

17.

18.

19.

20

My VIP Dream List

Your purpose in meeting the people you admire is to improve and invigorate yourself with what you learn from meeting them.

1.
2.
3.
4.
5.
6.
7.
8.
9.
10.
11.
12.
13.
14.
15.
16.
17.
18.
19.
20.

WRITE YOUR LIFE'S MISSION STATEMENT

"Nobody will have the same impact on history as you will." - Stacia Pierce

Once I started living my life by my mission statement, I began to make more accurate decisions that lead me closer to fulfilling my goals and purpose in life. I have never been more satisfied with my life than I have been since I began to live out my mission. Knowing your mission will help you to know how to act, what to do, how to dress, and what to say when challenging situations arise.

A mission is defined by Webster's College Dictionary as "a specific task that a person or group of persons is sent to perform." It is also described as, "an allotted or self imposed duty or task; calling." Most women are not living our their life's mission or "calling." As I have traveled the country doing book tours and women's conferences from my book; *25 Ways Women Can Motivate Themselves,* I have encountered many confused and unfulfilled women. When I mention the subject of purpose,

27

and fulfilling your life's mission, the audience slides to the edge of their seat, and many questions arise. Therefore I know there is a common need for women to find true meaning in their life. Thomas Edison said, " I never did anything worth doing by accident, nor did any of my inventions come by accident. They came by work."

You have a God ordained mission for your life. In Jeremiah 1:5 (NIV) it tells us that God had a specific plan for our life before we were born. The scripture says, *"For I know the plans I have for you, plans to prosper you and not to harm you, plans to give you hope and a future."*

You're probably thinking, why go through all the trouble to create something as simple as a mission statement. You need one because of all the benefits:

1. It increases the value of your life.

2. A mission statement will reveal to you who you really are.

3. *It's a written statements of purpose and behavioral boundaries worthy of life's pursuits and it will determine the things you most care about doing in your life.*

4. *It will help your think creatively to solve your problems when internal and external obstacles come to stand in the way.*

5. *A mission statement allows you in difficult times and crisis to fall back on the realities of who you are and what you stand for, in respect to your responsibilities and obligations.*

6. *It will provide a balance in your life and a fulfilling way of doing what you're called to do.*

7. *It can stimulate you to think and assess yourself against the opportunities that are available.*

8. *Your mission will give you drive as you nurture it daily.*

9. *You will not be happy unless you are working on your life's mission on a daily basis.*

10. Having a personal mission statement will help you know what type of relationships you need.

11. It will help you with time control. You'll begin to know what activities to engage in and what activities to eliminate.

Once you start working on your mission, you no longer have a job, but a purpose. You are doing something you love and believe it or not, someone is willing to pay you to do it. I discovered that your mission will continuously unfold and expand, but you still stay true to your calling. I was so relieved to discover throughout the word of God, that God's will for any believers life's is never something that they don't like to do or something they are not good at.

A good mission statement is easily communicated and isn't long. It should be big enough to encompass your entire life's activities. I have a one sentence mission and I also have a one page mission outline for my life, family and church. Your mission will fit your particular interests, gifts and will perfectly coincide with your personality. Most people can't find their mission, because they don't take the time to know themselves.

Do a Personal Assessment:

Look at your gifts, your likes and dislikes and you will begin to draw a conclusion on what your life's mission is. Mrs. Fields began baking cookies in her home. She really enjoyed baking and as more and more people wanted them, she went on to own a store in the mall and is now a successful entrepreneur. Mary Kay Ash of Mary Kay Cosmetics, wanted to help women make money while being at home. Plus, she also wanted to improve women's self-esteem. So she started a direct sales company and is now one of the richest women in America.

Once you have gone through the natural process of outlining your life and discovering your uniqueness, do your spiritual work next. Prayer is always the best way to get the appropriate answers for your life. Through daily communication with God and prayerfully seeking Him about your calling, the Holy Spirit will begin to reveal and unfold your life's mission. Joshua 1:8 tells us to meditate in the Word day and night... *"This book of the law shall not depart from your mouth, but you shall meditate in it day and night, that you may observe to do according to all that is written in it. For then you will make your way prosperous, and then you will have good success."*

31

God's best is that you have good success. Your success comes from being in the will of God. When I was working on writing out my life's mission statement, I asked God to give me direction for my life, and show me what problems I was created to solve. I have has strong sense of purpose and direction in my life since the age of 13, so this wasn't an extremely difficult task for me. It was more of a process for fine tuning and getting specific. So within about three weeks of diligently seeking the Lord I had written my personal mission statement.

The time it takes you to fine tune your mission may vary, but you can get a general outline in just a few days. Don't procrastinate, but sincerely make it a goal to write out your life's mission statement immediately.

Indentifying Your Mission

✎ Write down as specifically as you can the description of the group, kind or type of people you want to serve. What interests you? Politics, women's issues, men, children, the rich, the poor, education, travel, family issues, art, fashion, etc.

✎ Write down the means by which you will help people. Describe a few of the talents, gifts and characteristics you plan to use: i.e. writing, speaking, designing, creating, planning, organizing, leading, teaching.

✎ Write down what you want these people to achieve through your help? I.E. good products, excellent service, motivation, direction, happiness, spiritual growth and increased knowledge

✎ Write down several action verbs that describe what it is you want to do to help others. For example, study, motivate, create, provide, give, reach, teach heal, build, educate, produce, launch, design etc.

Here are a few questions that helped me, and will help you pin point your mission in life.

Idea File:
Questions for Mission Clues:
Record the answers in your journal

1. If you could teach three things to others what would it be?

2. What do you deeply enjoy doing?

3. What are the three most important things to you?
> a.
> b.
> c.

33

4. What talents and gifts do you have?

5. When you look at your personal life, what activities are your greatest works?

6. How could you convey what excites you?

7. Who do you feel called to help? It could be a group or a cause.

Example: women, men, children, family, singles, church, leaders, entrepreneurs, business people, teachers, government officials, the elite, the down and out, youth, health & nutrition, elderly, etc.

8. What results are you currently getting in your life that you like?

9. What's causing those results?

10. What don't you get bored with doing?

Get started now and begin to write out your very own mission statement. Once you have written out your mission statement, place it somewhere visible so you can consistently be reminded of where you are headed.

My Mission Statement
Stacia Pierce

I will motivate ordinary women to live extraordinary lives!

I will awake daily excited about life and the opportunities that await me each and every morning.

I alone will choose those endeavors I wish to participate in and I will only partake in those things that move me closer to my destiny.

I will motivate my family to be their very best and they will be able to personally testify of my ministry.

I will contribute to establishing a fun, fulfilling and faith centered environment in my home.

I will provide the atmosphere and tools that will inspire my children to achieve greatness.

I will treasure my family and spend quality time building strong relationships with those closest to me.

I will live a Christian life of honesty and integrity.

I will bring positive change to the lives of those whom I influence and I will inspire others to greatness.

I will continue to grow by stimulating my mind with the word of God, ever increasing my relationship with God and continued new learning.

I will value the freedom of financial security that my profession and products will provide. I fully understand that freedom and financial security alone cannot provide happiness, but fulfilling my God given dreams (purpose) and maintaining my values will provide happiness.

I will do monthly substance and information checks to help me measure my progress toward my goals. I will pay close attention to my personal growth and assess my influences.

I will have a careful selection of people, places and events that I partake in.

I will impact the lives of 5,000 people on a weekly basis at Life Changers Christian Center- within the next five years, alongside my husband.

I will minister God's word through conferences, books, tapes and media throughout the world.

I will have a unique ministry to women encouraging them to have a close relationship with God, motivating them to fulfill their destiny and challenging them to improve their self-esteem.

I will use tools such as books, W.O.R.D. magazine, motivational tape series and my Women's Success Conference to motivate women to a higher level of living.

What's Your Mission?

⚑ My mission in life is to:

_____

⚑ Describe the type of people you will help

_____

⚑ You will help them by:_____

_____

So that:_____
(identify what these people will achieve with your help.)

3 SET TOO MANY GOALS

"Shoot for the moon for even if you miss it, you will land among the stars."

-Author Unknown

There are so many books on the process of goal setting. You can almost get confused if you read too many. I have simplified this whole process and developed a set of guidelines for effective goal setting.

A goal is what you specifically intend to make happen. It is not enough just to make a list of goals; you must develop a passion to want to see your goals come to pass. Colossians 3:23 tells us; "And whatsoever ye do, do it heartily as to the Lord and not unto men." I've never seen anyone achieve significant success in life without having a passion for what they were doing.

Once while I was ministering to a group of ladies, I challenged them to go home that night and write out "too many" goals. I told them to try fifty in just the area of their purpose, or the thing they have a passion for doing. The whole audience said; "Wow!" Their eyes got big and their facial expressions were as if I had just given them the biggest challenge they had ever faced.

I thought to myself, "This is a good exercise, because it's stretching them way out of their comfort zone." I knew it would be a big challenge because just weeks prior I had updated my modest list of twenty goals to fifty. Now, about a year later, I'm writing another fifty because many of my original goals have been accomplished. Every time you move up to another level of success, your mind automatically moves up to a higher arena of thinking, so you'll have new goals on the next level.

To live your life without any goals is to aimlessly walk through life. Goals give you a target. They are the "how to's" of all your dreams. Some of my goals have deadline dates, while others don't have a specific date, but I know that within a certain time period I want to accomplish them. This is why I have five year goals, ten year goals and twenty year goals.

Goals are the action steps to your dreams- they get you

up and moving. This past year I had a goal to complete three books (this being one of them). On the days I felt like calling it quits, my goals kept me motivated. It was like healthy competition. I wanted to win so I kept writing.

Without any life goals you cheapen the value of life, but with goals, you realize how valuable life is. Therefore, it is essential that you take the time and write down your life's goals.

God was into goal setting so much so that He gave His chosen servants life goals. Peter Daniels gives some interesting insight on goal setting as he outlines some men and women in the Bible who were given goals. For example:[1]

Abraham was given a life goal to father many nations, and it was promised under obedience that it would continue for generations to come.

Moses was given a life goal to deliver the Israelites to the Promise Land. Only at the point of delivery, was his life task completed.

🎖 Saul was made king and although he disobeyed God, was never harmed or even threatened by David, God's divinely chosen successor. Saul's anointing could not be removed due to the sacredness of his life's goal.

🎖 Hannah had a life goal for her son Samuel, and with God's help he marched through the pages of biblical history as a prophet, demonstrating his life's call.

🎖 Joseph was given a goal to be a provider for his people and his family. Through ridicule, suffering and opposition, he reached it.

Goal setting is exhibited throughout the whole Bible and serves as a guide and example of how we too should live our lives with a set of goals.

I am thankful for my father who introduced me to the concept of goal setting. He would tell me to write down what I wanted. I thought, "What an immature practice." That was my youthful, foolish thinking. Then finally, one summer I took his advice and created a goal list. It changed my entire life. I began to realize my dreams and make major progress in my life.

When I first had the idea to write books and become a serious author, I thought, "What's the use? It's so hard to get published." Then I recognized that I was hearing the voice of the enemy. The truth is, if you keep writing, you'll get published. The same holds true for meeting important people. You may think, "How will I ever meet these people on my VIP dream list." But if you keep doing what you're called to do, and you do it well; the right people will eventually want to know you.

So, don't aim low in your goal setting because of circumstances, other people's predictions, or your own feelings of inadequacy. Instead, aim high and make a move toward your goals immediately. When a goal is achieved you'll find great satisfaction in your accomplishments and gain great momentum.

Five Ways to Effective Goal Setting:

 1. Goals should be specific.

2. Goals should be challenging.

3. Individual goals will many times have to be linked to a group of goals. For example, my goals for women's ministry are linked to our church goals.

4. Goals should focus not only on the ends, but also the means.

5. Goals must be written down. If it isn't written it is not a goal.

 **Idea File:**

Write 25 of your own personal goals:
1.
2.
3.
4.

5.

6.

7.

8.

9.

10.

11.

12.

13.

14.

15.

16.

17.

18.

19.

20.

21.

22.

23.

24.

25.

I hope you took the time to fill in your twenty-five goals. This book is about moving from everyday existence to creating a life worth living. Life is so full of surprises and wonderful discoveries. I want to wake up your senses to all of the inventions of your own creativity that are within your reach.

BE EXCELLENT

"Get enough information and insight to do it right the first time."

-Stacia Pierce

Pay whatever price necessary to make yourself excellent. Excellence is what God wants for you. My definition of excellence is simply getting enough information and insight to do it right the first time. Dr. Ira Hilliard defines excellence as; "giving attention to details which causes a superior performance." From the first day our ministry began, our leaders have been taught to operate in excellence. I come from a very excellent background. In my former profession, before going into full time ministry with my husband, I was an image consultant. My job was to help managers, business owners, and employees develop personal excellence, which would transcend into excellence in performance.

I've learned that you must first develop excellence in the unsupervised areas of your life before it will come out for everyone else to see. We find this principle in Luke 16:10 which

47

says; "He that is faithful in that which is least is faithful also in much: and he that is unjust in the least is unjust also in much." Take care of the little areas in your life.

Develop excellent grooming habits. The way you care for yourself will have a direct affect on your self-esteem. Excellent grooming is shaving your underarms on a regular basis, keeping your nails well manicured, bathing daily. This may seem a little juvenile, but sometimes women can get into a grooming rut.

The condition of your closet, your car, the upkeep of your bedroom and bathrooms speak volumes about who you really are! Don't settle for an average lifestyle, but decide right now that you will pay the price to have superior non-compromised living.

It will take a little extra effort to possess this above average lifestyle, but the results are worth it. Excellence attracts and gets the attention of uncommon people. I can recall being in Nordstroms in Seattle, Washington shopping for shoes. The sales lady was exceptionally nice to me and very accommodating. After I had picked up several shoes she asked; "Are you on T.V.?" "No," I said. "You look so nice and familiar," she responded. The lady was drawn to me simply because I dressed nicely. She figured that I must have been someone important. Often when you dress with excellence, and look like you deserve first class treatment, you will get it.

Ever since my children Ariana and Ryan were little, I made a commitment to dress them with excellence and purchase good quality clothes for them. I know that children are affected by how they look. Believe it or not, children as young as two years old are very image conscious. Dress your children in the best clothes you can afford. Always keep them looking neat and clean, unless of course they are in their play clothes. When your children are well groomed it is more likely that teachers, coaches, babysitters, and those who influence them will treat them with excellence.

Excellence means mastering the details which could

be boring and dull. It took me years of study and lots of reading before I began to call myself a motivational speaker for women or begin to write books with authority. I know that spectacular performance must always be preceded by unspectacular preparation. It takes a long time to become an "overnight" success.

Begin to prepare yourself in excellence for the area of your life that you want to shine in. There is more in you than what you are already doing. Evaluate yourself and make a list of the areas of your life where you need to become more excellent. Look around you, could you improve your wardrobe, your lingerie, or your home? When you are truly excellent you leave everything you touch better than you found it. It becomes more valuable since you touched it.

For example, the beauty of our home is partially attributed to the care of the previous owners who gave great attention to details. They put the best accessories you can find in our house. However, we are still upgrading our home and investing in it to increase its excellence and value.

Excellence proceeds preparation and practice. I'm a much more excellent writer today than I was when I wrote my first book. With each book I write I see my writing style unfold. My creativity has emerged and my word usage has expanded. I'm pleased with my latest works. This book in particular brings great pleasure because it is a climax to my last book *"25 Ways Women Can Motivate Themselves."* It takes you on a journey of discovery. Without my prior preparation of reading good books and personally practicing the principles that I outline in this book, this project wouldn't be excellent.

Hindrances to Excellence

There are negative attitudes that will hinder you from walking in excellence. You must identify, and overcome any hindrances that are holding you back. Below is a list of hindrances to resist.

Comparison

Constantly comparing yourself to others will always breed discontentment. Be excellent in what you are assigned to do. Don't worry about what someone else's course is in life. Remember, the best you can be is number two when you try to walk in someone else's assignment.

Poverty Mentality

There must be a renewing of the mind. When a person is unwilling to make the proper investment to receive the necessary gain they are being cheap. Excellence will cost you money. The Bible clearly tells us in John 10:10 that God came to give us life more abundantly. You will have to make investments in books, tapes, traveling and upgrading your surroundings. Don't allow a poverty mentality to abort your destiny.

Corrupt Communication

Ephesians 4:29 tells us: "let no corrupt word proceed out of your mouth, but what is good for necessary edification, that it may impart grace to the hearers." Your mouth can be your biggest enemy to excellence. Don't make statements like: "It doesn't take all that." "I can't afford it! I don't have the money." Instead begin to make faith confessions like: "My God supplies all my needs; I have more than enough." and "Money cometh to me."

Mediocre People

Proverbs 29:19 TLB tells us; "that a mirror reflects a man's face, but what he is really is, is shown by the kind of friends he chooses." When you surround yourself with people who are enemies to excellence, you will eventually lower your standards to please those who you associate with. The truth is most people admire excellence in others, but are not willing to pay the price to be excellent themselves. Begin to surround yourself with other significant people whose presence puts a demand on you to come up to another level.

How to Acquire an Excellent Presence:

Women that possess an excellent presence exude an aura of confidence deserving of attention and respect. Below are six steps you can take to improve your personal presence:

1. Stay on Top of Current Events

In order to sound intelligent you must have something intelligent to say. By reading informative (not garbage/gossip) news magazines and newspapers, your I. Q. will expand.

2. Read Books

If you don't read, your scope for learning and obtaining knowledge is limited. Did you know that your level of success can be measured by the books you read, the tapes you listen to and the information you learn from them?

3. Improve Your Vocabulary

Use proper English while communicating with others. Take time to learn new words. Study great speakers and learn their communication skills. Mark Twain said "The difference between the right word and the almost right word is really a large matter-It's the difference between lightning and the lightning bug."

4. Maintain Proper Hygiene

One of the greatest turnoffs is offensive body odors. Before leaving your home, do a personal hygiene check up. While traveling and working, keep a "freshen-up" kit with you.

5. Maintain Your Stamina Through Good Health Habits

By eating the right foods, exercising regularly, and maintaining a positive attitude, you will increase your ability to perform at your maximum potential while also improving your personal appearance.

6. Keep your Personal Assets in Tact

✔ Take a close look at your car. Is it clean and safe to ride in?

✔ Check the inside of your briefcase or purse. What does its appearance say about your organizational skills?

✔ Glance down at your shoes. Do they indicate that you are a well groomed person?

✔ Consider the cleanliness of your home? Are things in their proper place? Is it clean? What will others think of you upon entering?

 **Idea File:**

Practice being an excellent, extraordinary woman.

Extraordinary vs. Ordinary Women:

Extraordinary Women...	Ordinary Women...
1. Make time	Waste time
2. Say "Lets find out."	Say "Nobody knows."
3. Empower	Control
4. Do it	Talk about it
5. Are a part of the solution	Are a part of the problem
6. Are not afraid of losing	Are afraid of winning
7. Make commitments	Make promises

8. Work harder than an ordinary woman	Are always too busy
9. Learn from others	Resent others
10. Are continuous learners	Say "I've learned enough"
11. Say "I'll plan to do that"	Say "I'll try to do that."
12. Catch people doing things right	Catch people doing things wrong
13. Say, "I was wrong."	Say "It wasn't my fault"
14. See opportunities	See problems
15. Celebrate others	Complain about others
16. Give	Take
17. Translate dreams into reality	Translate reality into dreams
18. Expect success.	Expect failure.
19. Do extraordinary things	Do ordinary things.

Go through your house and give attention to all the details in your life. Look at your clothes, furniture, lingerie, carpet, shoes, closet and car. What things are a little off or are not properly fixed or organized? Do you have a shirt you always wear with a safety pin in it? Is their a old phone cord that needs replacing? How about a worn out shower curtain hanging mercilessly in the bathroom? Take the next thirty days to fix those things that are out of order.

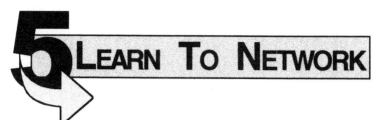

5 LEARN TO NETWORK

"When you're at the party, dance with the one who brought you, because you may need a ride home."
                                        -Harvey McKay

The concept of networking has taken on a negative connotation. Networking can be abused if a person doesn't use proper protocol, but networking is a way of life. No matter what goals you're shooting at, you'll need a network. When you look at networking for what it really is, you won't have that ill feeling when you hear the term.

Networking is caring about people, learning about them, listening to them, spending time with them, and paying attention to them. Networking is asking what you can do for someone else. It is not just about what someone can do for you. Networking is the process of making connections. Networking is searching for people with whom you can build a relationship. To have a good network, both parties must be willing to give and maintain the relationship. For example, right in the middle of writing about this topic, a Federal Express delivery

57

man came to my office door with a package for me. "Wow, what could this be?" I questioned. I knew that I hadn't ordered anything this week. "It looks like something special," the delivery guy teased.

After signing for the package, I immediately opened the box, curious to see what was inside. With the box open on my desk I released a great sigh, "YUM!" This is from a first class person, it's Godiva Chocolates." I grabbed the box to see who sent it...my friend Renee. I met Renee while at a women's conference a week earlier, where we were both guest speakers. We formed an instant bond when we met and we chatted throughout the week like gradeschool friends who hadn't seen each other in a while. I knew then that this lady would be in my network.

Renee owns a women's clothing store and due to our networking, she is now supplying the clothes for my fashion show-which is a part of a major women's conference that I host annually. Renee obviously knows how to maintain her network, because she followed up on our meeting with a very impressive gift. Not that buying people gifts purchases friends for you, rather it is what the gift says. Your gift denotes value, honor and caring. The gift you give a person tells them what you really feel about your relationship. You will have to put forth a little time, money and creative effort to cultivate good relationships. A good network can provide role models, service, advice, comfort, entertainment, social resources, financial assistance, and prayer, so it's important that after reading this chapter you immediately go to work on building your own network.

How to Go to Work: Build your Network, by Working on Yourself

Upgrade your skills, develop yourself and discover your strengths. You have to be able to bring something to the table. You also need to know what you're looking for in a network. The type of people you connect with will be dependent upon your mission in life.

Work on Your Communication Skills

Introduce yourself to new people, wear a welcoming smile and tell a little about yourself. Greet people with enthusiasm. Ask good, open-ended questions, so you can get the other person to elaborate. Learn new words so you can properly communicate your thoughts. Sometimes people don't want to listen because it's takes the other person too long to explain themselves. Try to meet people who aren't just like you. Harvey Mackay said; "If everyone in your network is the same as you, it isn't a network, it's an ant hill."

Get to Know Them

Get to know people better by asking the right questions. There is certain information you want to know about those in your network like:

🕊 What are their dreams, goals and values?

🕊 Where have they been?

🕊 Where do they want to go?

🕊 Who do they know?

🕊 How can you help them?

People in your network are a great resource in your life, so you want to find out what's important to them.

Update your Information File

As you get to know more information about the person you've added to your network, you may want to update their information profile with some personal information like:

🕊 The person's birthday

- The names and ages of their children, and if they involved in anything noteworthy?
- Their anniversary (if they are married)
- Their hobbies or interests
- Their favorite colors
- What the person does in his or her free time

This information can be very useful if you ever decide to buy a gift for the person.

Networking Strategies:

Go Somewhere

If you never mingle in any new circles you'll never meet any new people. Get out; go to a good women's conference. Attend your church sponsored events. I know a part of my purpose is to be a leader of leaders, to minister to other pastors' wives. Last year my speaking engagements greatly increased, which gave me the opportunity to meet many pastors' wives. This year alone, I have added over one hundred women in leadership to my network. There are only a few that I have close relationships with, but I try to keep all of them abreast of what's happening in my life and ministry.

Don't Look Over People

Learn to be down to earth. Never get too big for certain people. Granted, depending on your position, you won't be able to relate to everyone you encounter the same way, but you can always treat people nicely. Never act superior to others. You never know who God is going to use to do big things in your life.

 Relate to Your Network Based on Facts

Learn to distinguish between social acquaintances and an influential network. Some relationships will be just for business. Others, may just be for advice and mentorship, and then others may be for support and sharing a mutual friendship. Don't confuse them. Work within reality. The mistake that many people make is assuming there is more to a relationship than what really exists.

 Tools to Maintain Your Network:

 Calling Cards

I could have referred to these as your business cards. Whether you are taking classes, work for someone else, own your own business or are at home, you need calling cards. They are professional, easy to hand out, and people are less likely to misplace them. You can jot a personal note on them as well. Just think of how many times you met somebody new and wanted to exchange numbers. You probably ended up fumbling in your purse for a scrap piece of paper and a pen. This method of exchanging information not only makes you look unprofessional, but it causes unnecessary stress once you get home and try to find that little piece of paper you wrote on.

I once read a magazine article about a stay home mom who decided to make herself calling cards on her home computer. She came up with this creative idea after meeting other mothers on the playground (or elsewhere) and always forgetting their names. The calling cards were complete with her and her child's name, address home phone number and e-mail address. This is a perfect example of how calling cards are a simple, pleasant way to remember people you meet and have them remember you.

Roledex

Every woman should have a systemized way to maintain all of her valuable contacts. Challenge yourself to add one new name to your roledex each month. I have two roledexes. One with professional contacts and the other with personal contacts. Every once in a while I flip through it to see if there is someone I need to touch base with.

I'm now teaching my daughter Ariana the importance of networking. She has her own unique address book. She can place a photo of her friend in it, then write in all the vital information: favorite colors, hobbies or sports they partake in, birth dates, age, addresses and phone numbers. She's is getting a early start on her network.

Cards & Gifts

Keep a stock of "special day" cards on hand. If someone in your network has made an accomplishment, send them a card to show your support. I agree with Mike Murdock who said, "Never try to pursue a relationship with someone who tolerates you but doesn't celebrate you." A few weeks ago, a really nice article was written about me in our local paper, *The Lansing State Journal*. Excited, I called a few of my friends to tell them about it. My friends celebrated with me and were so happy that you would have thought that the article was about them. Be sure to celebrate those in your network, for there will come a day when you want to be celebrated.

Develop Your Trademark

One of my trademark ways of showing appreciation for my network is to send a card or gift when those closest to me accomplish something significant. Periodically, I'll send pictures of my family and update information about what's happening in our lives. Keeping cards on hand makes this an easy practice.

👓 Be On The Look Out.

You can't be close minded to who you may need in your network. Since my husband and I travel a lot, we have developed some really unique relationships. Included in our network are concierges, limousine drivers, hotel managers, restaurant reservation hosts, bank managers, editors, retail store owners, flower shop owners, Fortune 500 company presidents, political officials, travel agents, wholesale distributors, printing company owners, pastors and pastors wives, T.V. actors, singing artists, speakers, authors, and so many others.

This list is just to give you an idea of who can be in your network. Remember, all of these people do not have to be your best friend to be a part of your network.

65

Idea File

One of the best ways to implement a new idea into your life is to immediately take action within 24 hours after hearing the idea. If you don't already have a roledex, go buy one. Create a list of the ten most important people in your network right now. How have you kept in touch with them? Why are they important to you? How can you benefit them and they you? What are you doing to keep the network alive?

6 STRETCH YOUR MIND

"All men who have turned out worth anything, have had a chief hand in their own education."
-Sir Walter Scott

Push yourself intellectually. Begin to think above average. The Bible tells us, "As a man thinketh, so is he." This verse explains why those who don't think much, don't obtain much. Did you know that your mind is open to suggestions and it will grasp onto whatever you feed it? The majority of the people you will meet in your lifetime will only use half of their thinking ability.

Many times we as women keep our minds so cluttered with noise, leaving us little time to really think. When TV and radio consume the majority of your time, your mind will get accustomed to not wanting to think on its own. The more knowledge you have, the more confident you will be. To stretch your mind you will have to stretch yourself out of your comfort zone. Reading and listening to tapes daily may not be an easy task to adjust to immediately, but if you put forth a daily effort, you will be pleased with your results. I discovered that when we practice "limited thinking" about our own abilities, we will also think limited about the abilities of others. To oversee our staff, I had to stretch my thinking and creative problem solving capacity. Once I began to learn more and do more, I could lead them to learn and do more. I'm proud to say that our staff is a team of experts in their specific areas.

For example, one of our staff employees has had no formal education in marketing but she developed her gifts and stretched her mind, and submitted to our training. Now she is one of the best media marketing experts in the country. She has had several job offers by major firms, but she remained committed, not only because we take good care of her, but because she knows that we were responsible for getting her to stretch her mind.

I also had a similar experience with my daughter Ariana. A few years ago I challenged her to stretch her mind and listen to positive Christian tapes and set aside daily personal reading time. I also encouraged her to write letters to family and friends at least once a month and to keep a journal. The results I have seen in Ariana are phenomenal. She thinks on such a high level and has developed such a wittiness to solve problems. Her creativity has soared as well, and her confidence level is above average. It's all because she's doing and becoming more than she could have previously imagined. If parents don't stretch their minds, they won't encourage their children to stretch their minds.

Stretching your mind also involves having the ability to see old things in a new way. You need to stay open to new methods. Seize opportunities to learn and grow intellectually. I remember having a certain mind-set concerning the way women's ministry should be done . But as I began to get curious and collect bits of information, I stretched out of my comfort zone and became open to new methods and ideas. I also listened to tapes of other women who were in ministry. After a while, God ideas began to emerge. I would write them down and file them away, not knowing at the time that I would later be writing books, training and leading women's ministry.

Here are a few ways you can stretch your mind:

✔ **Read biographies, magazines, newspapers and nonfiction books.** Carry reading materials with you at all times so you can turn sitting time into learning time.

✔ **Spend time with well educated people-** especially creative people who are walking in purpose.

✔ **Set a personal development goal to become an expert in a field that interests you.** Gain all the knowledge you can about that particular field.

✔ **Stop the habit of watching too many videos or too much TV.** Don't waste your days or evenings. Instead, see a play or attend a ballet. Become more cultured and invest in forms of entertainment that will help you enhance yourself academically and socially.

✔ **Travel and visit a variety of destinations.** If you can't afford to travel to the locations you desire, purchase a book on the places you want to visit and begin to study them. This will motivate you to save for a visit.

✔ **Listen to informative tapes.** Use driving time or housecleaning time to become more informed.

✔ **Ask Questions.** When someone is talking about a subject that you are not familiar with, ask the person to explain.

✔ **Spend Time Alone.** Spend time in meditation on the word of God. Quiet time with yourself and God is one of the best investments you could ever make.

✔ **Read Your Bible.** Expand your knowledge of spiritual principles and how God operates.

✔ **Keep a journal of subjects that you have studied.** Make action notes of how you plan to utilize this in your life.

We live in an awesome time. More information is available to the public than ever before. There are so many opportunities for learning all around you. Dedicate this year toward personal growth. What do you want to become an expert in? Plan to experience life through seeing, reading and touching new territories over the next twelve months.

Idea File:

How to Stretch Your Mind
Step 1
I want to become an expert at:_____

_____

Step 2
List five steps you plan to take immediately to stretch your mind.

1.

2.

3.

4.

5.

Step 3
Name two well educated people you know who you can spend time with and glean information from.

1.

2.

Step 4
What type of seminars would you like to attend? List subjects:

1.

2.

3.

4.

5.

Step 5
How much money are you willing to invest this year to educate yourself?

_____

Step 6
Name one new location you would like to travel to:_____

Now gather all of the information you can about going to that location such as:

💰 Hotel expenses

✈ Travel expenses: (i.e. air fare, car rental, gas mileage, miscellaneous expenses)

💵 Spending money

⏍ How long will you be staying?

⛅ Weather/Climate

🏛 Tourist attractions, landmarks

Near the close of the year, I began to stretch my mind by thinking of projects that would be fun to do or books I would write if I had all the tools, resources and time. This journalizing exercise stretched me more than I ever imagined. I wrote "I will write a novel even though I have no experience in that kind of writing, nor have I had a desire to do so before." Once I put the idea on paper, a flood of ideas accompanied the thought. What seemed at first like a notorious idea began to consume me as being possible. Who knows what will come of my journal entry.

That is what stretching your mind will do for you. It will stretch you into unfamiliar territories, but it won't leave you there; it will cause you to actually live a more rewarding life.

COMMUNICATE WITH CONFIDENCE

"Perfect your communication skills: reading, writing and speaking and your confidence will rise."

-Stacia Pierce

Do you fear being called upon to give an impromptu speech or make an introduction of a very important person? Most of the women I have come in contact with over the years say that their biggest fear is standing in front of an audience. Why? Because they fear they won't do or say the right thing.

Even if you don't possess a fear of speaking in front of a crowd, it's always good to know how to communicate properly. Effective communication skills can be especially valuable when you are called on to make an unexpected presentation. There are so many women who are not fulfilling their dreams to teach a class, lead a Bible study, become a professional speaker or start a business due to feelings of inadequacy as it relates to communicating. The Bible illustrates how great men of God felt inadequate about their speaking abilities. In Exodus 4:10-14 when Moses was called by God and told that he was the one assigned to utter the words "Let my people go," he told God to send somebody else. Moses replied; "But Lord, I'm not a good enough speaker; I never have been and I'm not now - even after you have spoken to me, for I have a speech impediment." God responded; "Who made your mouth?" In other words, God was reminding Moses that He had created his mouth and certainly had the ability to place within that mouth the appropriate words to say. God didn't change Moses' purpose, He sent him away saying; "Since you insist, I'll send your brother Aaron with you."

In Jeremiah 1:4-10, God told Jeremiah he was appointed to be the spokesman to the world. Jeremiah replied, "I can't do that! I'm too young; I am but a youth." God firmly responded, "You will go where I send you and speak whatever I tell you to." He further instructed Jeremiah saying; "Don't be afraid of the people's faces; I will be with you to deliver you or to help you through it;" and after touching his mouth God said, "I have put my words in your mouth."

Confident women are secure in their communication skills. When the opportunity arises to conduct a meeting, make an announcement, give a speech or introduce someone, they walk confidently to the podium. The communication secrets I've learned which have caused me to speak confidently before people, are the same methods I have used to train my leadership team. The same principles will work effectively for you when you apply them.

Motivating Thoughts on Communication

Don't allow your youthfulness to cause you to speak timidly. Speak with boldness. Whether you are young in age or just beginning the effective communication process, don't be timid. I began public speaking at 19 years old and ran into a lot of resistance. I stood on Luke 21:15; "For I will give you words and wisdom that none of your adversaries will be able to resist or contradict.

Stay in God's will. When you are where God sends you He shows up with you. You won't be speaking by yourself. Have you ever felt led to tell a friend something but didn't know how to say it? What did you do?

Repeat what God has placed in your heart. Don't alter your message to please the people. Have you ever weakened a message because of what people might have thought? How did you feel?

Have your thoughts organized. It's okay to use an outline or notecards, this will help you stay on track and keep you focused.

Don't be intimidated by faces of skepticism. There is no need to be afraid of the people. If they knew what you knew, they would be the ones speaking, not you.

Speak with confidence knowing that God has placed a unique message in your mouth.

Practice speaking. To be a good speaker, you should rehearse and practice in front of a full length mirror. Take advantage of every opportunity to speak.

Read engrossingly. Try consuming a book per week. Read a combination of books, magazines, and newspapers, especially about the subjects you plan to speak on.

Learn a new word each month. Write the word and it's definition. Practice using it in sentences. Take every opportunity to exercise your vocabulary. Incorporate the new words you've learned in your conversations.

Be eager to stand before an audience to speak.

Listen intently to great speakers. Note their style and how they deliver a message.

Record yourself when you do speak and critique yourself. Listen to the words you use to make illustrations and explanations.

Invest in a good dictionary and thesaurus. Utilize them to research words, understand their meanings, and know how to use them correctly.

Avoid the overuse of faddish words and slang. It limits the scope of the message to the social group that it is derived from, which compromises it's effectiveness.

You must realize that communication is a necessary tool to being a confident woman. At some point you will need to communicate your thoughts, dreams, desires and plans. When women lack communication skills they lack living a full life. There's so much to say and so much to be done, but the truth of the matter is, we need somebody to hear what we have to say and someone to help us reach our goals.

7 Power Points for Effective Communication

1. Don't Be a Bore. Prepare a presentation that even you would like to sit through.

2. Be Prepared. Prepare for an opportunity that does not yet exist. You prepare by thoroughly knowing your subject. Do your homework.

3. Create Your Own Introduction. Give the person introducing you a bio to use.

4. Know Your Mission. Be clear on the message you are trying to convey and why. Talk about a subject that you know about.

5. Only Use Humor That is Appropriate.
Don't use jokes that are offensive.

6. Be Natural and Have Style. Just be yourself without pretense; people like authentic speakers.

7. Record Every Presentation. Always get a tape recording of your presentation and listen to it a day or two later. You will become a great speaker if you keep evaluating yourself.

Over the years in ministry, I have grown tremendously in my communication skills. How I started however, is another story. I tried to implement the communication style of other women in ministry whom I thought were prominent. With time and maturity though, I began to master my own unique style of communication. People like you best when you're simply being yourself.

If you feel you have a message to share, the best way to prepare is to gather as much information on your subject as possible. Next find mentors who are already speaking and teaching. Buy their tapes and books. Study the things that make them successful. I've been speaking for years now, but I still try to listen to an hour's worth of teaching from another speaker each day. Not only does it build my faith, it also keeps me current to what God is saying and doing in the life of others. Almost daily, ideas come to me which aid me in fulfilling my purpose. I believe it is a direct result of reading and listening to inspirational tapes.

Communication Update Alert...
Why you need to
be technologically
updated:

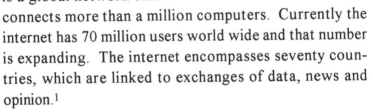

Everywhere you look these days
you're are told to visit a web
site or find what you need on
the internet. The web and
the internet are not the
same thing. The internet
is a global network that
connects more than a million computers. Currently the
internet has 70 million users world wide and that number
is expanding. The internet encompasses seventy coun-
tries, which are linked to exchanges of data, news and
opinion.[1]

The World Wide Web is a part of the internet. It's a system of specially designed documents called (pages or sites)
that support links to other documents, graphic audio, and
video files. It gives you the ability to go from one document to another by simply clicking your mouse on a link.
Get involved in this new way of discovering knowledge,
doing business and communicating with clients and friends.

Internet access gives you the ability to obtain extraordinary knowledge on just about any subject, in a short period of time. There is so much information on what the internet can do for you, that I could write a whole book just on that subject. Do some research on your own, and stay updated and alert to life. Before long, to contact just about everyone you know, you'll have to remember their phone number and e-mail address.

It is essential that you become communication literate. We are about to embark upon a new way of communicating in the 21st century. Every household needs a computer with internet access.

There are many new digital devices on the market today, but we should have our homes equipped with the basics. The following are a few. Fax machines make it easy to instantly send a document. They only cost a few hundred dollars for such a convenience. E-Mail is an electronic mail service which you use on your computer with a modem. It's great because E-mail is a non formal way of communicating. You can be brief and to the point. One of the newest exciting gadgets is a Motorola Page Writer 2000-a digital pager that can receive e-mail.

The Card Scan 300 will process all your business cards

that you will collect from networking. You may be comfortable with the old way of doing things and may question whether all of this is really necessary. But the truth of the matter is the world is rapidly moving forward with new technology and new information daily, and if we don't keep up, we will be left behind. Our kids are growing up in a new era, and as parents we have a responsibility to be educated about what will influence them.

There are several new books coming out about the new technology and how it all works. It would be highly beneficial for you to read up on the subject. Plus, there are all sorts of computer classes offered at community colleges for a minimum cost.

We recently purchased Web TV in our home and in just a few days our entire family became experts on how to surf the web. At Christmas time, I looked up all the toys and books I wanted to buy and researched the products in the comfort of my own home, while sipping hot tea and eating a scone. I saved hours of shopping time and sore feet, so for me, the new way of communicating has many bonuses.

# Idea File:
Let's Get Technical

Get an e-mail account.

Get a name and address. Should you choose an internet provider, E-mail accounts usually come as a part of your initial package.

Choose an internet provider.

i.e. America On Line, Explorer, or you could do what we've done and get Web TV.

You may want to create a website.

If you plan to be self-employed or have a business, you'll need a website. A well designed site can provide lots of information for your clients and an easy way to advertise. You may need to find a website designer to help you.

85

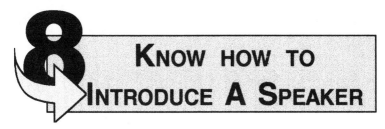

KNOW HOW TO INTRODUCE A SPEAKER

"The paradox feared by every presenter is that it takes considerable preparation to be spontaneous."

-Bob Gerald

I have been to conferences where the host never said a word to the audience, they just had a very vocal person communicate their messages for them. This behavior demonstrated a real lack of confidence in the host. People usually are afraid that they will sound ridiculous or worry about what the audience will think of them. However, this chapter will help you deliver your introduction properly and with confidence.

I was introduced once and it sounded ridiculous. The commentator said; "This is Stacia Pierce who has a long list of credentials one of them being, she is a motivational speaker. Let's welcome her as she motivates us." Wow. Now I had to spend five minutes explaining to the audience who I was, where I was from and why I was qualified to be the speaker at that event.

Whenever introducing someone, there are a few rules that you should follow:

A few "Rules of Thumb" for a proper introduction:

1. Spotlight your Speaker

John the Baptist was a biblical example of someone who had to make an impactful introduction. He had the awesome responsibility of introducing Jesus. He had to prepare the way (John 1:23) and break down the wall between the speaker and the audience. When John took the platform to make his introduction, he decreased, so that the speaker could increase.

2. Be Prepared.

In advance, ask the speaker for a written bio. Review it long before you get up in front of your audience. Do more than read a bio if you can. When making your introduction, add notes to your comments about the speaker. Keep it very brief. If you know the speaker, add some exciting personal comments.

Plan an effective presentation by answering the following questions:

-Who: The speaker's name

-What: Talents, abilities, credits and honors
           he or she has attained.

-Where: Is the speaker from?

-Why: Is the person best for this occasion?

3. Present enough information to establish credentials.

Tell why the speaker is qualified to speak on their subject. Never put a speaker up without saying anything. If the speakers have products for sale, always endorse their products. The host usually has the greatest influence with the audience, and should use it to the benefit of the speaker they have invited.

4. Hold your head up high.

When it comes time to walk before your audience to give the introduction, hold your head up and walk confidently to the podium. You should be interesting and positive, brief and enthusiastic. Remember, always take a humble posture when introducing a speaker, and keep the emphasis on them.

"Everyone has butterflies in their stomach. The only difference between a pro and an amateur, is that the pro has the butterflies in formation!"

-Zig Ziglar

"As you anticipate living an extraordinary life, know that there will come a time when you are called upon to make an announcement. Today, every woman should know how to communicate publicly, whether at the family reunion, your church, your wedding reception, or any other social gathering."

5. Keep the Group Alive.

To avoid a "dead audience" when making an announcement, ask yourself: "What am I trying to say? Does anyone need to hear it?" When making an announcement be expressive, articulate and well spoken.

6. Learn Eloquence Before You Are Put on the Spot.

* Make your announcement clear. Answer...

-Who: Is sponsoring the activity?
-What: Is its plan and purpose?
-Where: Is it located?
-When: Is it scheduled?
-Why: Is it important to attend?

Tips

☐ Make your announcement positive. Don't say anything negative. Emphasize only the positive points.

☐ Purchase a good book of quotations for your reference library. A quotation can add validity to your announcement.

☐ Be brief. Nobody will remember a long, drawn out announcement.

☐ Make it complimentary. Don't make an announcement that put's a person on the spot negatively.

☐ Choose colorful and expressive words that will paint a picture in the head of your audience that will stick with them.

☐ Project your voice clearly and loud enough so that everyone is able to hear you. Don't mumble a soft spoken announcement because no one will pay attention.

☐ Look up. Make eye contact with your audience as much as possible.

# Idea File:

Presentation Primer

"Prepare yourself for an opportunity that does not exist yet."

Pretend that one of your friends is a guest speaker for an event you are hosting. Interview your friend and write a one page bio or introduction. Practice introducing them in their presence. You may want to record this exercise so you will know how you sound. After your presentation, ask your friend to critique you.

Remember:

Who:_____

_____

What:_____

_____

Where:_____

_____

Why:_____

_____

KNOW HOW TO HAVE A SUCCESSFUL MEETING

"The secret of success is to do the common things uncommonly well."

-Sprat

Meetings are a valuable communication tool. When organized properly, meetings generate synergy causing everyone involved to focus on a unified goal. They are a tool of motivation. I have a few different groups I meet with each month. My women's leadership team meetings are approximately two and a half hours and my staff meetings last about an hour unless we are strategizing on an issue. Our family also has meetings which are held periodically throughout the year. Regardless of the type of meeting or the length of time, I try to keep all of our meetings exciting and full of purpose.

Every successful meeting begins with a plan. Never begin a meeting without a specific, well thought out plan. Review and rehearse your meeting notes so you will be confident when it's time to perform. Failing to prepare, is preparing to fail. Here are the guidelines I use to conduct a successful meeting:

☒ Always create a written agenda. It should include:

📄The date of the meeting

📄The subject heading

📄The goals to accomplish

📄 Points to discuss

📄Any expected task from the participants

☒ Choose a good day. I found that meetings held later in the week are more productive. Usually on Mondays people want to get caught up or focus on the upcoming week.

☒ Be unpredictable, your meeting should be creative and adventurous.

☒ Be creative. When you make it fun for people to come to your meetings you'll get a lot more commitment, energy and enthusiasm.

☒ Show enthusiasm. Your voice, actions and words must express delight in the subject you are covering. Remember to smile.

☒ Avoid any social chit-chat and drifting off on one point for too long. Stick to the agenda and watch your time.

☒ Resolve any disagreements immediately. Stay in control of the meeting. Don't allow personal agendas to interfere with the overall purpose.

☒ Watch the nonverbal clues of group members for signs of confusion, resentment, boredom or alienation.

☒ Always bring your calendar along. If it is necessary to schedule another meeting or give deadlines, you can do it then instead of getting back with people later.

☒ Speak with authority. When Jesus spoke, the people were astonished with his doctrine, for he taught them as one having authority and not as the scribes. (Matthew 7:28-29). Jesus spoke with authority because he knew what he was talking about. Know your information!

☒ Summarize the following at the conclusion of your meeting:
　🏆 The accomplishments
　🏆 The goal
　🏆 The group's commitment
　🏆 Their expected action steps

For the success of any company or group of people trying to work together, meetings are necessary for communication purposes. Without a plan, meetings can be notorious time wasters. That's why I have done everything possible to make sure that my meetings are both productive and exciting.

# Idea File:

Pretend you have to meet with a group of people who are assisting you to make your dream come to pass. Use the meeting agenda on the next page to plan your meeting.

Meeting Agenda

Place:_____

Start Time:_____Ending Time:_____

Purpose of the meeting:

_____

Desired outcome of the meeting:

_____

Participants: (Who needs to be there?)
1.
2.
3.
4.
5.
Goals and Objectives: (What will be discussed?)
1.
2.
3.
4.
5.

Tasks Assigned
<u>Assignment</u>   <u>Party Responsible</u>
1._____
2._____
3._____
4._____
5._____

PART II:
LOVE

PROMOTE SELF-ESTEEM IN YOURSELF AND OTHERS

"The greatest good we can do for others is not to share our riches, but to reveal theirs."

-Author Unknown

The Bible tells us in Proverbs 23:7 that as a man thinketh in his heart, so is he. How you think in your heart will determine your self-esteem. I'm not just talking about positive thinking, but Bible thinking-getting your heart in line with what God says about you. Many women today are stifled in their ability to go to the next level because their self esteem is not intact. Did you know you are a supernatural, divine creation of God? Creating a good self image, by seeing yourself as God sees you, can set you on the path to becoming the person you've always desired to be.

Five Steps to a Positive Self Image

1. Get a New Image of Yourself:

See yourself as an overcomer, achiever, and prosperous in-dividual. Make all the necessary natural changes to feel good about yourself. Up grade your hair style, dress neatly, smell good, and walk like you are someone special. You have to believe you are special before anybody else will.

2. Destroy the Old Image

Speak to your negative thoughts and cast down every evil imagination of your old self. You are not what you used to be. Be careful not to destroy your future with negative images of the past. It's good to analyze the past but don't be paralyzed by it. After my first marriage and going through a divorce, I remarried. In the first few months of my marriage the enemy tried to fill my mind with the old image of that failed marriage. I had to renew my mind by using the word of God. I wasn't the same person, neither was I married to the same kind of person. My future was bright.

3. Deal with Your Problems Head On

The characteristics of someone with low self-esteem are usually laziness, procrastinating, gossiping, exaggerating, or constantly being critical of others. If you suffer with any of these traits, admit it to a trustworthy person and repent.

104

4. Keep a Positive Confession About Yourself.

Remind yourself of the qualities and values that you have. Don't snare yourself with negative self-talk. Boldly profess positive things over yourself. I write out my prayer confessions and speak them out loud daily. This is a good way to be consistent.

5. Encourage Yourself in the Storms

Storms will come, and trials will come, but don't allow them to ruin your self-esteem. Know that it will pass and things won't always be as they are. Thoreau once said; "If you drive confidently in the direction of your dreams, you will meet success in the unexpected hour." You are a spectacular woman, so don't become weary in well-doing. You will surely reap if you faint not!

Promote Self-Esteem in Others:

God was always promoting self esteem in others. God told Gideon he was, "a man of valor," although Gideon thought he was the poorest and the least in his father's house (Judges 6:15 AMP). God promoted self-esteem in Joshua when he told him, "Be strong and of good courage..." because he was important and he would cause the people to inherit the land (Joshua 1:6 AMP). Promoting self-esteem in others is a positive communication tool that you will need to possess to live an extraordinary life. A good mentor will always promote self-esteem in others. As a pastor's wife and leader, I had to learn the value of imparting into others. You get the best results from people who feel good about themselves and good about you. Plus, when you promote self-esteem in others, you start to build more meaningful relationships. People always ask me, "How do you get the ladies at your church to assist you?" The secret is that I promote self esteem in them. If you are a leader over a group, some of your peak performers may be limiting their effectiveness simply because they don't realize how important and special they are as people.

Become an Encouragement Coach.

Encourage everyone you come in contact with to become more.

Help other women set exciting and specific goals for their professional, personal and spiritual development.

Be committed to helping them get started with implementing those goals.

Celebrate the victories of others by documenting their successes in written commendations.

106

🐝 Excite other women around you with opportunities to grow through training, education and mentorship with you. Just share the knowledge you have, and keep growing yourself. Challenge others to improve their performance by the life that you live.

🐝 Be generous with compliments

🐝 Thank people personally when they achieve something important.

🐝 Whenever you get a good report about someone who is a subordinate to you, tell them.

🐝 Catch someone doing something right and tell them they're caught.

Idea File:
Promoting Self-Esteem Exercise:
Write a list of people with whom you have influence and whose self-esteem you can promote (i.e. husband, wife, children, friends etc.).

1._____

2._____

3._____

4._____

5._____

Now write out what you can say or do to boost their self-esteem.

1._____

2._____

3._____

4._____

5._____

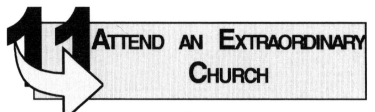

11 ATTEND AN EXTRAORDINARY CHURCH

An extraordinary church will cause you to rise above common level.

-Pastor James Pierce

To be an above average woman, it is vital that you be plugged into a extraordinary church. Sometimes we down play the role that church can play in our success. I'm capable of writing on this subject since my husband and I pastor an extraordinary church. I also have traveled to speak at many other churches and can spot an extraordinary church immediately. There are some key components that make up a good church.

I can remember meeting a very gifted lady who had a real heart for the things of God. She talked about her goals, dreams and how much she wanted to make a great contribution to others. Sadly, she belonged to a church that didn't build her self-esteem or feed her the type of messages from the word of God that she needed to soar. During a conversation, she admitted her reason for staying saying,

"I know that I can only grow so far at my church, but my family goes here, so it must be meant for me to stay." I replied; "I would really pray about my spiritual growth if I were you." It's sad, but this is a classic case and so many women have the same story. The secret to your success is found in the word of God and the church you attend.

Your church plays a significant role in you fulfilling the will of God in your life. For example if you are single, and a man approaches you concerning a relationship, your priorities should be as follows: does he take where he attends church seriously? Does he attend regularly? Does he financially support the church? And so on. These issues are going to come up once you are married, so it's better to resolve them while you are still single.

If you are married then you can't decide alone where you attend church. If you feel like your husband is comfortable in a church that is not causing your family to grow, go to God in prayer about the situation. When you feel that it is the right timing, ask him to visit another church that is teaching the word of God. There are some key components that make up a good church, I've outlined them below.

Six Traits of an Extraordinary Church

1. The Pastor Must Walk in Integrity.

The character of the leader must line up with the word of God. I Thessalonians. 5:12 tells us to know them that labor among you. This does not mean that you should know the Pastor personally. Yet it does mean that you should know what your Pastor stands for. You can't rise much above the level of your leader, and you won't be able to grow and prosper. If their life is in shambles, chances are yours will be too. The Bible gives us a description of how a pastor should live his life in I Tim 3.

2. The Pastor Must Have a Big Vision

If you want to do extraordinary things in your own life then you need a church with a big vision. The Bible tells us in Proverbs 29:18 that without a vision the people perish. You want to be in an inspiring environment that pushes you towards perpetual growth. An extraordinary church will stretch you out of your comfort zone.

A Pastor with a big vision will give hope, direction, and a future to those who follow him. If you belong to a church where the Pastor has a big vision, do your part to help the vision come to pass.

3. A Church That Teaches the Word

When you are in a church that gives you knowledge of the Bible and understanding, then those biblical principles can be easily applied to your life. You'll be amazed at how quickly your life will improve. You should need a Bible at church; that's a sign that the minister is planning to teach you something. You should also be encouraged to read the Bible for yourself. II Tim 2:15 tells us; "Study to shew thyself approved unto God, a workman that needeth not to be ashamed, rightly dividing the word of truth."

I can recall when I first attended an extraordinary church. I was living in Atlanta Georgia, and a friend asked me to go to a meeting to hear Marilyn Hickey. Upon my first visit to this church, I could tell there was something different. Even during the offering, the Pastor talked about walking by faith and not by sight. I thought; "Wow, that's motivating and gives me hope for my future." I knew immediately that I wanted to be around these people and hear more about faith. Hebrews 11:1 says; "Now faith is the substance of things hoped for and the evidence of things not seen." An extraordinary church will show you how to operate by faith to do extraordinary things.

112

4. A Commitment to The Great Commission

Matt 28:18-20 tells us to go out into all the world and witness. You want to be a part of a soul-winning church- the kind of ministry that cares about winning the lost and is doing something about it. Some churches have become cliques that don't want to grow or win any new people to the Lord, because it might "mess things up." Most people's excuse is " We want to be intimate and small." How self- ish , when we have a whole generation of people who are lost and will go to hell if we don't reach them.

5. A Powerful Worship Experience.

There should be an emphasis on worshiping the Lord in song and praise. The songs should build you up and be biblically sound. A church doesn't have to have an entire live band to have a powerful worship experience. More importantly, the music should lead you to focus on the Lord.

6. Excellent Children and Youth Ministry

The type of children's ministry a church has will often de- pend on the age of the church. You want a church who at least has a plan to minister to the children and youth. The children should be taught the word of God on their level. Many times your children will learn things in church that will have a dramatic, positive impact on their life. When we started our church, we immediately made plans for children's ministry, even though we didn't have many workers at first. We grew the ministry little by little. We kept the vision for a stand-out children's ministry before our people weekly. Then after awhile volunteers began to come forth, and we did lots of training. We also spent money to send our leaders to other ministries to be trained. Now our children and youth are excited about coming to church each week.

7. Promotes Fellowship

There should be some activities you can get involved in to meet new people and fellowship. Today, people want a church that becomes a part of their lifestyle- not just a place to worship on Sundays. We have ministered to hundreds of college students who say that our church was the first one that they actually stayed at any length of time, because there was so much to do. We kept them busy so they didn't go back to their old lifestyle. Men's, Women's, Singles' and Married Couples' fellowship groups are a good place to connect with people. Home care groups are also good for fellowship and growth. So look for a church that promotes fellowship.

What kind of member should you be?
1. A Regular Attendee
In order to benefit from your church you have to be there. You should be faithful in your attendance. Don't let church be an option. Faith cometh by hearing, so you must hear the word taught on a consistent basis.

2. One Who Gets Involved
Donate some of your time to the church. Find an area that you can help out in, even if it's just cleaning up things weekly, or working in the nursery. Attend your church sponsored events like conferences, workshops, special meetings, etc. Go to the fellowship groups. They are put in place for your benefit. When you do get involved, adhere to the church guidelines. Most churches have a 'ministry of helps' guidelines.

3. One Who Contributes Financial Support
Tithe a tenth of your income into your church. Then give

an honorable offering as well. Support building funds and special programs. The only way the church can keep winning the lost, is by the support of the members. Buy every book and most of the tapes that your Pastors release. Not only does this show your support, it helps you to grow into a mature Christian.

4. One Who Speaks Positive Words

Never talk about your church or its leaders. If you are in a good church you may not understand every single thing that happens. However, as long as you are being fed the Word, keep a positive confession about your ministry. You hinder your own blessings when you curse others with your mouth. Plus, if you have children and they hear your negative talk about your church, you teach them to be skeptical and critical, too.

Relating to Your Pastor's Wife

Your pastor's wife is a gift from God to you. She is an extension of the pastor. She is his help mate; so she helps equip him to be able to minister effectively to you. The women in our church are wonderful. They go out of their way to accommodate me and make me feel appreciated. I have never had a problem with not being treated with respect since the conception of our ministry. My husband has done a wonderful job of establishing just how I should be treated.

But I have counseled several pastor's wives who have felt unappreciated and even disrespected by the members of their church. So it's apparent that women need to be educated on how to treat a pastor's wife. The Bible tells us to do unto others as we would want it to be done unto us. A good rule is to treat your pastor's wife in the same manner in which you want to be treated. Her position calls for her not to be your personal friend or your personal advisor, but for her to assist her husband in ministry in the way that works best for them and his vision.

5 Ways You Should Treat Your Pastor's Wife
1. Honor Her
Spiritual authority is somewhat similar to political authority. Take our president and his wife for instance. Though the president's wife doesn't have equal position as her husband, she still fills the honorable office as First Lady. The same holds true in the church. The pastor's wife is the First Lady; meaning she should be the number one honored lady in the ministry. Even if there are other women in the church that are extremely gifted, in full time ministry or over departments, no other woman should receive more honor than the first lady.

2. Sow into Her

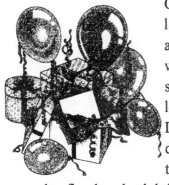

One year for mother's day the ladies in my church inquired about the fragrance of perfume I wore, my brand and color of stockings, and what kind of body lotions I preferred. On Mother's Day they gave me literally hundreds of bottles of perfume, lotions, stockings and bath products plus five hundred dollars to use for lingerie at my favorite lingerie store. It was simply overwhelming. It was such an act of love and kindness. Because of the way they sowed into me, it opened my eyes to just how much they were paying close attention to me. It stretched me to want to become the best pastor's wife they could possibly have. Remember your pastor's wife on Mother's Day, birthdays or when she has a baby.

One year Dr. Leroy Thompson ministered at our church a message called "Money Cometh." He revolutionized our church and taught our people how one way they will get increase is through sowing into the man and woman of God. He suggested, "The next time you give them a card, put some money in it." Since that day, my husband and I hardly ever receive a card that doesn't contain some type of monetary expression as a gift. So I pass that advice on to you. As you act on it, watch how blessed you will be.

3. Respect Her

Regardless as to whether she ministers or not, respect your pastor's wife. When other female speakers come in to minister at your church, you should celebrate them, respect their office and even let them know how much your enjoyed them. Everybody likes healthy, positive feedback. But it would be disrespectful to compare another ministry gift to your pastor's wife. Next, respect her by keeping your contact with her husband to a minimum. Yes, he is your pastor and you honor him for helping you change your life around, but you have to be careful to show your appreciation in moderation and with tact.

4. Assist Her

I have four women who are trained pastoral assistants called P.A.'s. These women have served in our ministry for a long time and have been very faithful to the church and to the things of God. My pastoral assistants help me before and after ministering, with my children and when I travel. I also have twenty-five women on my women's leadership team, who assist me with women's ministry. Your pastor's wife may need your assistance, but if she doesn't know you very well, you may need to assist from a distance.

Offer to run errands for her or provide a service. If you are in the book store and you see a book that would interest her, buy it for her, to save time.

5. Support Her

If your pastor's wife hosts a women's fellowship of any kind, show your support for her by attending. If there are tickets or registration fees, pay them early. Don't procrastinate until the last minute, then it looks like you don't really care about the event. Remember if your pastor's wife is hosting an event, it's for you, not her. Hundreds of women from my church, take off work, usually using their vacation days to support my annual May women's conference. Because the conference is so educational, many companies will now pay for employee's to attend.

 # Idea File:

If you are a member of a church, buy your pastor's wife a present and put a note with it sharing how much you appreciate her. Find out what your pastor's wife really likes, so you can sow into her things she will really use.

12 LOVE YOUR HUSBAND

"Women, learn to treat your husbands as kings; every king needs a queen."
-Mack & Brenda Timberlake

A fresh and exciting marriage is one to be admired. You can greatly contribute to making your marriage sizzle and making your husband feel loved. James and I have an excellent relationship, but it does take work on both of our parts. I have always loved my husband and he has always loved me, but as we matured we learned to express our love in many ways.

I set a goal to be a wife to be admired by my husband. My husband and I believe that there is always something you can learn about marriage, so we have attended some very good marriage conferences. Every year we listen to tapes and read books on marriage so we can constantly improve our relationship.

Love your husband enough to make personal improvements on yourself. Contrary to popular belief, studies show

show that most men want a wife that is intellectually stimulating. Especially if the husband's career causes him to stay on the cutting edge of new thoughts and trends. You should strive to be an interesting person for yourself and for your husband. You should be able to hold productive conversations with your mate and give keen insight or creative ideas from time to time.

 One year I read three church growth books because that's what my husband was studying at the time. He would come home and begin talking about improvements and strategies for our ministry. At first I had no idea what direction he was trying to go in. So I read the same books he read, and they gave me awesome insight. Afterwards, I was equipped to hold an intelligent conversation about his interests at the time. Plus, I could actively support his vision because I was in tune with it. You will only grow intellectually if you allow yourself to be curious. Take out time to read, study and listen to tapes. Commit to loving your husband by developing yourself.

6 Ways to Love Your Husband

♥ 1. Stay in Good Health
To be sick all the time can become burdensome to another individual. Granted, there may be conditions that

may come upon you that you have to believe God for healing, and it may take some time to recover, but for the most part, do what you can do to stay healthy. Eat light, especially if you plan to be intimate with your mate soon after eating. Lose weight if necessary, you want to feel confident about your body. Get enough sleep and exercise so you will be energized. Drink water daily. I always suggest to every newlywed to read the book; *Fit For Life*[1] It will open your eyes on how to stay healthy and live a long time.

♥ 2. Laugh Together

Good times together create a strong bond. My husband and I have so much fun together. Our home is a happy home. We laugh a lot, watch comedies together, discuss funny incidents, and engage in activities together that cause us to laugh. Shared activities, play and laughter can improve even the best of relationships.

Dr. Harley said a man's need for recreational companionship is second only to his desire for sexual fulfillment. So find ways to have fun together. You don't have to wait for your husband to initiate all the romance or adventure; you do some creative planning.

♥ 3. Dress for Him

Wear clothes that will make your husband proud of you. Find out what he likes to see you in. When I first got married, I was a very faddish dresser. I wore dress clothes that were a little on the hip-hop side, so it made me look young. Well, I was very young. My husband wanted me to wear more suits and look a little bit more refined. The picture in my head of refined was that of dowdy looking navy suits with no pizazz, so I fought him about changing my style for about a year. Then we went on a shopping trip to New York. I found clothes that fit my style and bought some very colorful, embellished suits. When I'm dressed nice, I make him look good as well. Men want a wife they can be proud of, so go through your closet and take inventory of what clothes your husband likes or dislikes.

124

♥ 4. Buy Lingerie

Take a good look in your lingerie drawer. Are you behind the times? Often after women have children they trade in their sexy undergarments for nursing bras and white comfortable underwear. But after a period of time, you should return to fashionable undergarments. Try to keep up with the underwear fashions. Push up bra's, sheer underwear and the return of lace is on the scene now. It would be a good idea to have a complete lingerie wardrobe.

If you are behind the times when it comes to underwear, rush out to your nearest lingerie boutique and see what's in. For starters, pick up a pair of nice panties and matching bra and see what your husband thinks. Remember that men are turned on by sight.

♥ 5. Honor Him

Never put your husband down in public or in private. My husband and I don't totally agree on how to handle every issue that comes up, but I honor his spiritual authority. I honor him as the head of our home. So I have to bite the bullet sometimes. We have a very liberal relationship. In our private time, I freely voice my opinions and he welcomes.

that. However, I do not try to lead him.

Giving honor to your husband causes him to trust you. Proverbs 31:11-12 describes a virtuous woman. It says; "The heart of her husband doth safely trust in her, so that he shall have no need of spoil. She will do him good and not evil all the days of her life." When your husband knows you will only do him good, then he will trust you with the secrets of his heart. Speak well of him, not only to your children, but to others as well. You can cause your husband to be respected by others. Proverbs 31:23 says that the husband of a godly wife is respected at the city gate. He is respected in the community because of his wife's good report of him.

♥ 6. Encourage Him

What does your husband need from you? My husband has a big vision and is doing so many dynamic things for the kingdom of God, therefore he needs my support and encouragement. I try to compliment him after every message he teaches. I keep him encouraged as he takes on new projects. I listen to my husband's tapes over and over

126

again. It encourages him that I get blessed by his teachings even though I live with him. As a wife, become a chief encourager to your husband. Avoid criticism and sarcasm. That can destroy a marriage because it causes bitterness and resentment to set in. When I teach on the subject of marriage to our women, I tell them not to let another person encourage your mate more than you. Be sure to outdo everybody.

Idea File

*Every year commit to reading at least one marriage book. A few excellent choices are *Life Savers for Your Marriage* by Mack & Brenda Timberlake and *Your Husband, Your Friend,* by Bob Barnes.

* Think of a way to show love to your husband this week.

13 LOVE YOUR CHILDREN

"If you bungle raising your children, I don't think whatever else you do well means very much."

-Jacquelyn Kennedy

Most women would say without hesitation, "I love my children." But even though we as mom's know we love our children, how we communicate our love sometimes sends a totally different message to our children. Loving our children is about celebrating the uniqueness in each child and providing an atmosphere that fosters healthy self-esteem as well as the freedom to fulfill their potential.

I have two children- a girl and a boy. They each have different personalities, so we have to make sure that we don't compare them. Instead, our emphasis is to guide them according to their personality types. Ariana is a choleric, which means she's driven, goal oriented, a leader and very opinionated. Whereas my son Ryan is more sanguine, so he loves being the center of attention, thrives on praise and loves to talk. With these inherent traits in mind

129

we have to express our love for each of our children in a different way. Here's some easy strategies I use to show my children I love them.

Practice One On One

The best way to develop individual relationships with your children is to spend time alone with each one on a regular basis. Many times I'll take Ariana grocery shopping with me or to a movie and out to lunch. We often have tea alone or write letters together. Ryan is still a baby, so I sit him on my lap and read a book to him, or take him outside in the backyard to slide or play in the yard.

Let Them Express Themselves

Most kids grow up with a fear of really expressing themselves around their parents. You should allow your children to express feelings of anger, hurt or resentment. Of course they need to be taught how to do so in a respectful manner; but just like you have feelings, so do your kids. Allow your children to talk about their feelings. Then guide them as to what they should do about the way they feel.

Develop a Bedtime Ritual

Before I had a routine for my children, going to bed each night was like pulling teeth. Now we have a ritual that the children actually look forward to. It includes taking a bath, a healthy snack, a short play time, a bedtime story or writing in their journal. After a brief discussion, a prayer and then a hug, the lights go out. Once your kids are in school, you should set a reasonable bedtime and stick to your schedule. As your child sleeps, whisper in their ear, "I love you."

Meaningful routines provide stability for your children. It makes them feel significant. During our brief talk with the children before they go to bed, my husband or I listen to their thoughts and ideas. Then we always tell them we love them. Say something positive and meaningful. "Like, tomorrow you're going to do a great job on your test because we prayed and you studied." or "I'm proud of your behavior today."

Once your kids hit their teenage years your rituals may have to change to thirty minutes before bedtime for family discussion time, where you can gather in a room with no TV interruptions for meaningful conversation.

Talk and Listen to Your Children

If you would set aside time for meaningful conversation, your kids will talk. You must talk on their level, though. Don't intimidate them with all your rules and regulations. They need to be able to be open and honest with you about what's going on in their world. You must engage in the conversation like what they're saying is important. Then, provide them with easy solutions.

Touch Your Children

Express your love through touching- hug them, and kiss them on the cheeks. Appropriate touching is an essential part of healthy development for boys and girls. I make a conscious effort to touch our children in the morning before they start their day and at night before bed. Then throughout the day I hug and kiss on them. Jesus knew the value of a touch for children (Mark 10:13-16 NKJV).

Show Your Love with Family Vacations

It's important that you save up your money so that you can take your children on a real family vacation. What do I mean by real vacation? I mean go beyond the visit to a relatives house. Visit a new state, country or place they've never seen before. Plan a vacation that's centered around your children and the things they like to do.

Every year we take a family vacation or two with another family. This vacation is geared toward the children's enjoyment. In doing so, we are saying to our kids; "You're a very important part of this family and we want you to enjoy life also." Last year we took an East Coast vacation visiting Washington D.C., Philadelphia, New York and New Jersey. Though I coupled our vacation with my book signing tour, the entire week was dedicated to the children.

133

We saw many sights that will definitely help them in school like the Liberty bell, Betty Ross' house, several museums, The White House, Arlington Cemetery, Wall Street, Statue of Liberty and several museums. We also ate at superb restaurants every night.

We even rented a limousine in New York just for the kids. It took them through Central Park, all over New York and our last stop before retiring was Ben & Jerry's for ice cream.

Idea File:

Think of a new way you can show love to your children this week. Plan time with each child over the next month to allow them to express themselves whether it be in conversation, a game or a special outing.

14 STRIVE FOR OPTIMUM HEALTH

"Prepare for the future by choosing to live a vibrant life today."
-Stacia Pierce

You can't be much of an extraordinary woman if you are always sick and tired. Sickness and disease is a burden to you and those closest to you. Sickness can steal your destiny right from under you. It can slow down your progress. On the other hand, good health can lift your spirits, and boost your energy. It can relieve aches and pains, giving you a new outlook on life. I know it's not easy to schedule in the dentist appointment, your yearly physicals, change that eating habit or begin an exercise program. Yet it's worth your effort to take care of your-self, plus you become a help instead of a hindrance to the ones you love.

We live in a generation now, where you will have to take your health care into your own hands. Today the emphasis is on a healthier lifestyle and preventive care. Not too long ago, I was experiencing some pain in my breast area.

After a few days of reading up on breast pain, I did a self examination and felt two knots in one of my breasts. Immediately I called my doctor and had a breast examination followed in a few weeks by a second breast examination and a mammogram.

Waiting for the results of the mammogram caused my emotions to be fragile. Before I got the call from my doctor with the results, a letter came from the breast health clinic to see a specialist. The letter triggered immediate thoughts in my mind that I had to cast down. Finally three days later the phone rang and it was the doctor with my test results. She said, " You're clear, your test results were negative, nothing showed up. But we have to do a routine follow up at the breast clinic. That's the only reason why you received a letter." I took a deep breath and released a sigh of relief. Still, I had a little anxiety about the routine follow-up. A week later I went to my follow up appointment. More tests were done and the breast specialist confirmed that the problem wasn't at all serious, but I knew that I should make some health changes to prevent it from being serious. I left with more confidence, but I knew that is was time to create a top notch health plan for myself and my family. Now, I needed to mix my faith with the proper actions to stay healthy.

Today, getting the best health care requires more than just following the doctor's orders. You have to become more aware of your body, how to fight diseases and what treatments are best for you.

Find The Doctor for You

Make sure that your doctor's values and communication style match your needs. Does he or she listen to you? If you believe in alternative medicine or herbal supplements, find out if she is open to incorporating them into your health care. My primary care doctor attends my church and is on my women's leadership team, so I know that we share many of the same views on health care.

Get the Facts on the Medication Prescribed to You

Ask the pharmacist for full information each time you get a new prescription filled, such as:

1. What is the name of the drug and what is it supposed to do? What are the benefits?

2. How, when, and for how long do you take the medication?

3. Are there side effects and what should you do if they occur?

4. What other medicines or activities should you avoid while taking this drug?

Get a Medical Journal

Write down any health problems you may be experiencing like headaches, sleeplessness, sluggishness, aches, etc. Keep record of your medical exams and take your journal with you to your doctor's appointments.

Get Regular Physicals

You should have a full physical exam at least once a year. You may need to have them every six months depending on your medical history. The exam may include, blood pressure, breast examination, pap smear, pelvic examination, and a cholesterol test. Some blood tests may be needed.

Get Sufficient Rest & Sleep

Most people need to get seven to eight hours of sleep each evening. You should have a regular bedtime. It has been said that sleep depri- vation translates directly into lower immunity. People with chronic insomnia often suffer from chronic diseases. When you create a pattern of going to sleep at the same time each night and waking up at the same time, your body will perform at it's optimum level.

Exercise Regularly

Try to include at least 30 minutes of walking three to four times a week. Even moderate exertions is beneficial com- pared to not exercising at all. I try to walk either outside or on a treadmill at least three times a week.

Eat Nutritious Foods

Most of your daily intake should consist of fresh fruits and vegetables and whole grains. Drink plenty of steamed dis- tilled drinking water.

Take Supplements Daily

Certain supplements can actually supercharge your body's defenses. I take 400 units of vitamin E a day along with

1000 milligrams of vitamin C, 25 milligrams of vitamin B6 and in the winter months, also Echinacea which is a cold fighting herb and Barley Green. Buy yourself a good vitamin and herb book to decide what you need for your body and check with your doctor or nutritionist.

See Your Dentist

You should have your teeth cleaned every four to six months. This will prevent you from having any serious gum disease. My mother just recently had to have some permanent teeth removed. Her dentist told her that if she had flossed on a daily basis, the problem could have been corrected. Zig Ziglar said his dentist told him once, **"Only floss the teeth that you want to keep."** I want to keep mine, so after hearing that I went out and bought floss picks and started using them immediately.

Keeping your teeth cleaned and flossing daily doesn't just cause you to have a pretty smile, but it can even help to prevent cardiovascular disease. In one study, at the University of Michigan school of Dentistry researchers found that patients 68 and older who had their teeth cleaned at least once a year were five time less likely to have strokes than those who had less frequent cleaning.

Clean your toothbrush. The moist environment of toothbrush holders can become a habitat for germs. Weekly, clean your toothbrush and holder with hydrogen peroxide.

Allow Fresh Air In
Open your windows so you don't keep breathing in, the same old stale air. For winter months use a humidifier for your home to help with breathing, especially at night.

Walk by Faith, Not by Sight
Believe that God is a healer. Focus on the positive not the negative. Talk about being healthy and whole not about sickness and disease.

Simple Solutions to a Stressful Day
Stress will affect all areas of your life, including your health. Sometimes as women we allow our responsibilities to overwhelm us. Instead we should enjoy each day. I don't allow myself to become stressed out. Instead when I feel that my life is getting busy and work is a little chaotic, I stick to biblical principles that reduce stress. All these principles can be easily incorporated into your daily lifestyle.

Slow Down and Be Still

Psalm 37:7 says, "Be still before the Lord and wait patiently for him." Psalm 46:10 says, "Be still and know that I am God." Commit to being still daily for a personal time of prayer and meditation. Remind yourself to slow down and enjoy life.

Live for Today

Many people walk in fear of the future or worry about yesterday. Don't worry about what happened in your past or what could happen in your future. That doesn't excuse you from planning for your future, but plan to have a bright future. That alone will alleviate stress.

Stay Around Upbeat People

Negative people will drain you of your energy, dumping on you loads of un-belief and problems. Rid yourself of those toxic relationships. Find upbeat motivated people - people who laugh and are excited about life. The Bible tells us that a merry heart doeth us good like medicine.

Practical Things You Can Do to Unwind

 Pour a calming cup of herb tea

 Put on soothing music

142

Take a bubble bath

 Enjoy a serene mood with scented candles

 Pamper yourself with a foot soak and foot massage

 Take a nap

Prayer

Commit to daily prayer over your life and body. Confess the word of God. Make a daily health confession. A sample of the one is following. You can pray it daily.

Health Confession

Father in the name of Jesus I apply the blood of Jesus over myself and my family (speak their names) and over our lives today. Holy Spirit, I trust you to give me utterance in the Spirit as I Pray over my body. I pray now in Jesus name: Every valve of my heart functions and pumps the blood to where it is needed in my body. My circulatory system is functioning properly. My blood is clean and free from any disease of infection. My brain functions at optimum capacity. My DNA is perfect the way that God designed it. I curse every cancer cell, tumor and growth that may try to attach itself to my body in advance. I take authority over it now in the name of Jesus Christ. I break any generational curse or anything that tries to pass through the bloodline in Jesus name. Father I decree your Word over my body. You Word decrees that: The memory

143

of the just shall be blessed. I thank you that my mind is blessed. I thank you that it is renewed and thinks on things that are pure, holy, just, honest and of a good report. Your Word also decrees that wisdom preserves life. Lord I thank you that you will continue to give me wisdom to take care of this temple that houses your Holy Spirit. I thank you that I will be mindful of what I eat, drink, how I sleep and what I do, so that your Word can bear fruit in my body. Your Word declares that mans days shall be 120 years. I declare this Word over my life and over the lives of my family members (name them), in Jesus name, Amen.

Idea File:

* Get a complete physical.

* This month begin to build yourself a fitness and nutrition library. Start by reading: *The Bible Cure* by Reginal Cherry M.D., *Fit For Life* by Harvey & Marilyn Diamond and *The Christian Women's Guide to Health and Nutrition,* by Stacia Pierce.

*Make an appointment for something you haven't done in a long time. In the next 24 hours, call your doctor, dentist, gynecologist or nutritionist.

* Take a trip to a health food store, not a commercial type that is usually found in the mall, but an independent one.

15 ORGANIZE YOUR LIFE

"Dost thou love life? Then do not squander time, for that is the stuff that life is made of."

-Ben Franklin

In order to fulfill your dreams in life you will have to live out an organized life. Extraordinary women have a systematic way of running their lives. After writing out my dream list and looking over my list of responsibilities, I knew if I was going to achieve extraordinary success, I'd better quickly adopt an organized pattern in which to live by. You must adopt a system for the way you run your life.

Sometimes I'm asked if I feel overwhelmed with responsibilities? No I don't, because I have organized my life and I walk in God's rest. If you are feeling overwhelmed today with responsibilities ask God to make Matt 11:28 real to you. "Come all ye that labor and are heavy laden and I will give you rest." One of the first ways to put your life in order is to get all of your plans out of your head and get it on paper! Don't try to trust your memory.

5 Ways to Think on Paper
1. Keep a Journal

Become a buyer of empty books! Whenever I see a journal that appeals to me, I buy it because I know eventually I'll run out of paper in the one I'm currently using. Fill your journal with valuable ideas that come to mind. Often book titles or messages come to me in the middle of the night. I wake up and record the information in my journal so that I can refer to it at the appropriate time. Your journal will help you organize your thought life. Besides, your wit and wisdom is worth recording. Read my points on journalizing in my book *25 Ways Women Can Motivate Themselves.*

2. Keep a Project Binder or Folder

In a three ring binder or file folders, keep a running account on all your projects. If you are remodeling your kitchen, keep all receipts, invoices and important phone numbers that relate to the remodeling project. Create a project folder for each of your children. Keep any papers you have to fill out and return in the folders. I'm the director of special events for our church, so I keep a labeled color coded labeled file folder for each event and place any information I gather in it. Anything I need to work on a particular project goes in that particular folder. Once the event is over, I file away the important information and then delete the folder.

3. Use a Day Planner

Find a planner that is thin, light and easy to carry so you won't feel bogged down by it. My women's leadership team bought me a lightweight fuschia planner by Kate Spade for Christmas. It's the best planner I've ever had.

Begin to use your planner faithfully. Even if you don't know what to put in it, just start carrying it with you everywhere you go. Put all your reminders for scheduled appointments, bills to be paid, and a list of your dreams and goals in it. Fill in any important phone numbers. Use your planner at church, workshops, meetings or seminars to take notes and record ideas. Each day write something in your planner that you will do to move closer to realizing your dreams.

4. Use your Prayer & Purpose Planner

I would suggest getting my Prayer and Purpose planner to write your dreams and goals in and to post your faith photos. By consistently updating your planner and using it daily in your prayer time, you'll be reminded to stay focused. You will organize your life to head in the direction of fulfilling your purpose. Once you start using your Prayer

& Purpose Planner, you'll begin to recognize all the resources around you.

5. Live by a "To-Do" List

There will never be enough time to do everything you want to do. You'll have to choose what you do. Mike Murdock accurately states that: "Whatever you do in life you will have to trade time for it." The best time to plan is the night before. I try to write about six things I want to accomplish the next day. I found that when I plan the night before, I unclutter my mind.

The most successful people consistently make good choices with their time, so I make it a practice to carefully choose how I'll spend my day. Your daily agenda is your life. Make every day count. Protect your schedule from useless activities like too much T.V., too many phone conversations and excessive entertainment, etc.

Ecclesiates 8:5 says a wise man's heart discerneth both time and judgement. You have to discern how to use your time wisely. According to a study by the University of

Michigan, the average American adult spends their day as follows: eight hours of work, eight hours of sleep, two hours of eating, two hours of commuting, and one hour of personal hygiene. That leaves about three hours a day to do all the other things that you enjoy.

Look at your extra time over a week. If you don't work on the weekends, you should have an extra twenty hours in addition to the usual three hours a day. That's about thirty-five hours each week to develop your life. I said all of that to say that if you are going to spend your time wisely, then you need to spend it doing the things that you value the most.

Be Active

Organized people are active, productive people. They get a lot done in a day. I've learned to keep moving. I move quickly with pep in my step. It keeps me in a state of readiness. Being a self-starter isn't easy, because it requires you to be active even when you don't feel like it. Successful people do the things that need to be done-whether they want to do them or not.

Proverbs 6:6-8 tells us to look at the ant and learn about productivity. It reads; "Go to the ant you sluggard, and consider her ways and be wise. Which having no guide, overseer or ruler provideth her meat in the summer and gathereth her food in the harvest." The ant is a perfect example of staying active, because the ant doesn't need a coach in order to get the necessary things done. There's an old adage that says, "When you want to get something done, ask a busy person." To some extent that's true. Most of the women I know who are busy already with families and possibly working are the ones who achieve most of their goals without sacrificing a well balanced life.

Develop Extraordinary Routines

The secret of your future success is hidden in your daily routines. Routines can be positive when you engage in the right ones. When you do something at the same time each day or week you will save and generate energy. Routines mean your subconscious mind knows in advance what is going to be required. It will be consistently getting ready for the command while you are doing something else. Several years ago I began to incorporate routines that have caused me great success. I believe if you use some of them you'll get the same positive results.

Hair Appointments: Once a week at the same time and same day, I get my hair done. I bring along books to read or any project I'm working on, so I can get two things done at once.

Closet Care

Monthly, I do a closet checkup. I aim to have all the hangers in my closet exactly alike. I keep everything in uniform. My clothes are arranged in categories: Suits, pants, jackets, skirts and gowns. From there they are arranged by color.

Nail Appointments: Every two weeks, at the same time and on the same day, I get my nails done early in the morning.

Paying Bills: Once a month, I sit down at my table and get out all my bill paying tools. I utilize about an hour in one day to pay all of our bills for the month. Then I'm done until the next month.

Writing Letters:

I believe staying in touch with friends is important, so my daughter and I take a Saturday afternoon once a month to write all our letters.

Sleeping: Unless I am attending a conference or have just returned home from traveling I go to bed at the same time each night. When your body's clock is on a schedule, it makes you healthier and more alert.

These are a few of the routines that I abide by:

Rise Early

I Samuel 29:10 "Wherefore now rise early into the morning with thy masters servants that are come with thee. And as soon as ye be up early in the morning, and have light depart." Extraordinary women seize their day. They usually get up early. You will be amazed at how much you can have already accomplished while others are just starting their day. Mary Kay Ash is an extraordinary woman and she talks about how she belongs to the 5:00 am club. She encourages women who sell her cosmetics to wake up and begin their day at 5:00 am so they can accomplish their dreams and goals without it taking away from their household maintenance.

Enlist Help

Don't feel guilty about getting help. You don't have to be Superwoman. So many women struggle with trying to be good at everything that they miss being experts at what they are called to do. You have a purpose in life; you were created to do something special. When you are not fulfilling your purpose, there is an emptiness, a void on the inside, a tug that

152

reminds you that there is more to life. Don't burn yourself out trying to do everything. Get some assistance so you have time to fulfill what God has created you for.

Areas where you may need assistance are: cleaning, yard service, childcare and cooking. I use assistants in all of these areas and it has freed up my time to have dates with my husband, to travel, to do more with my kids, to write books and fulfill my purpose in life.

Develop Positive Organized Habits

Discipline is the refining fire by which talent becomes ability. I agree with Thatcher who said; "Look at a day when you are supremely satisfied at the end. It's not a day when you lounge and do nothing, it's when you've had everything to do, and you've done it."

Idea File:
Implement these 10 winners' habits:
1. Keep a daily journal.

Monitor your life experiences, your daily routines and effectiveness. Record your ideas and you'll see what direction your life is headed in.

2. Read a self-improvement book monthly.

It will give you a great competitive advantage.

3. Limit Your TV time

You could lose sight of achieving your purpose while watching somebody else achieve their purpose.

4. Read Your Bible Often

A consistent, repetitious Bible reading plan will give you the information and inspiration you need to keep your life on track.

5. Take Your Vitamins

Vitamins increase your energy level. When you have more energy, you are more productive.

6. Eat an Apple a Day

Apples are a great immune-building food.

7. Limit Phone Conversations

Remaining on the phone too long will rob you of all your spare time.

8. Write it Down

Commit your memory to paper. Always keep a pen and paper with you at all times. Be a good note taker. Capture ever intriguing thought or suggestion you get when you hear someone speak.

9. Plan Your Day The Night Before

You'll have a peaceful sleep and a productive day.

10. Begin to Replace All of Your Hangers to Look Alike

If you like your clothes, when your closet is uniformed, you'll find joy in getting dressed from now on.

16 DEVELOP A KNOCKOUT WARDROBE

"When a girl feels that she's perfectly groomed and dressed she can forget that part of her. That's charm. The more parts of yourself you can afford to forget the more charm you have."

-F. Scott Fitzgerald "Bernice Bobs Her Hair"

Your clothing talks and tells about your attitude, accessibility and ability. What are your clothes saying about you? Are you portraying the image you really want? Is God glorified in your clothing and appearance? If someone had to describe what kind of person you were solely by evaluating your clothes, what do you think they would say?

Those thought provoking questions should stimulate your thinking about clothes. What you wear is sending a message. Extraordinary women are confident women who have their self-esteem intact. Your clothes are just a reflection of what's going on in your life.

I believe in balance. Having a knock out wardrobe doesn't

157

mean you sacrifice food for your children, paying a house note, or worse yet, using your tithes
and offerings. But it does mean that you
dress your very best for the level you are
on.

My clothing choice changed as the seasons in my life changed. As I increased in
income and exposure, my tastes and
wardrobing needs also changed. I wanted
clothes that were durable, easy to iron,
looked great every time I wore them and
fit perfectly to reflect my personal style.
So I began to purchase some well made
clothes and designer lines. I also began
shopping at boutiques and stores that could
service me, not just sell to me.

In Exodus 28:2 when God appointed Aaron to be high
priest (the spiritual leader) He said; "And you shall make
for Aaron your brother sacred garments (appointed offi-
cial dress, set apart for special holy services) for glory
and for beauty." God wanted special clothing made to
indicate Aaron's separation to Him; showing that Aaron had
been elevated to a new office (beautiful garments that gave
dignity to his work). Even God is concerned about our appearance, though many religious minds would say otherwise.

Go to work on building your knockout wardrobe. First, determine what your clothing style is, then look for quality over quantity when shopping. You want to have a wardrobe of clothes that you really like and feel good in. Haven't you ever put on an outfit that you thought you didn't look good in, but you decided to wear it anyway? All day long, you were probably self-conscious about how you looked - standing back, not speaking up, walking with a slump, pulling and tugging away at your clothes, etc. That's why it's important for you to always wear what you feel good in.

When you want to change the level you are on, change the clothes that you wear! Every year I have an image enhancement course for all of the new ladies that have joined our ministry. In addition to the course, they have the opportunity to audition to be in our big fashion show in May. The show concludes our annual *Women's Success Conference*. After the women complete the course they testify about how prior to the course, they really didn't think clothing choices, makeup and image improvement mattered. However, they found out that it changed their entire perception of themselves. Many women take on new ventures that prior to the image course, they felt inadequate to do. The course lasts for 90 days, but it only takes forty-two days to create a new lifestyle. As a result, these women complete this course with a permanent, new and improved look.

159

Top 10 Ways to Change Your Look:

1. Buy the most expensive clothing that you can afford. Remember, quality over quantity.

2. Find your own style. It's the key to looking great!

3. Find clothes that reflect your purpose and call in life.

4. Unless you really know what you are doing, don't mix and match suits.

5. Invest in quality shoes: They can make or break an outfit.

6. Remember, casual days aren't tacky days. You can dress down but still maintain a polished style.

7. Invest in quality jewelry to accessorize your clothes. Your choice of jewelry usually adds your signature to an outfit. Accessories should be in proportion to your real size. Example: tiny jewelry and small sized scarves make large people look larger, etc.

8. Correct your posture. Stand with shoulders back, head tilted upward. Keep your abdomen muscles in, and press your pelvis in.

9. Upgrade you hairstyle yearly. A new hair cut can instantly improve your entire image. When you feel good about your hair, you usually feel great about yourself.

10. Feel your Best: When you look good, you feel good. When you feel good, you do good!

"To Do"

1. Educate yourself in the area of your image.

2. Set some wardrobing goals for your life.

3. Dress like the people you want to build rapport with.

4. When speaking before an audience, always dress a step above the crowd.

5. Buy at least one good fashion magazine a year, so that you're not totally oblivious about what's in and what's out.

6. Remember, with every level of increase or promotion, your image should improve.

7. Perfume your body; find a signature scent. Proverbs 27:9 says, "Perfume and incense bring joy to your heart."

8. Spend lavishly on your undergarments. Feeling feminine is a self-esteem booster.

Remember daily image habits determine your image outcome.

Taking Care of Your Wardrobe

The way you care for your clothes will also determine how they look on you. You may need to start with cleaning out your closet. There is nothing worse than a disorderly closet. It will cause you much frustration and hours of lost time over the years. My dress clothes and suits are organized by color, all red, purple, black, etc. hang together. My casual clothes are grouped by type: all pantsuits, then shirts, then slacks and finally blazers are hung together.

You may want to develop a system to keep your closet organized, because it will save you a lot of time and energy. I use clear plastic containers with lids to store my shoes. The shoes I wear the most are hanging on my closet door on a shoe tree. All my jewelry is categorized. My jewelry containers are separated into groups of gold, silver, colors, and black. My purses are lined up on the top shelf of my closet. I keep my underwear sets together in cute little storage bins in my closet. Now, getting dressed is a wonderful, hassle-free experience. You may want to

162

adopt some of my organizing techniques or come up with your own creative solutions. But whatever you decide, keep your family's closets organized and clean. This systematic way of caring for your wardrobe reduces the stress of getting dressed. Especially on Sunday mornings.

Fabric Fundamentals:
How to care for your clothes

Wool
Cleaning: Although wool is a stain-resistant fiber, you still need to treat a stain before it sinks in. Use a clean, damp sponge and blot, don't rub. Dry clean as little as possible; once a season should be fine unless heavily worn.
Tips: Wool retains it's shape if folded carefully or hung on padded hangers. Needs air and space to breathe. A steamy bathroom will remove most wrinkles.

Cotton,
Cleaning: If you are worried about shrinking, wash cotton in cold water; otherwise it can withstand very hot temperatures. Avoid over-bleaching, because it can wear down the fibers; every other wash is fine. Or try using white vinegar as a milder alternative to bleach.

Tips: Takes longer to dry than most fabrics, so use a hot dryer setting and touch-test until dry. Some 100% garments should be laid flat to dry to avoid shrinkage. Responds well to a hot iron, and doesn't easily scorch.

Tencel
Cleaning: Hand, machine-wash or dry clean, but check the label; manufacturers may add finishing touches that can affect that care.

Tips: Drip dry. Stable, holds color and maintains flowy character very well.

Silk
Many washable and colorfast silks can be gently washed in lukewarm water. Keep the wash cycle short and rinse quickly. Never use chlorine bleach, and don't let garments soak for long periods in water. If you dry clean silk, be certain that the label recommends it; some silk dyes react to solvents.

Tips: Hang dry if woven; dry flat if knit. Protect from light, air and insects.

Polyester
Cleaning: Dry clean or machine wash.

Tips: Dries fast. Use permanent-press cycle and remove as soon as possible to prevent wrinkles. If needed, iron on low setting only.

Cashmere

Cleaning: Hand wash in cold water with baby sham-
poo or detergents formulated for delicate fabrics. If high
quality, the long, soft hairs in cashmere actually become
more luxurious with each hand-washing.

Tips: Lay flat to dry; use cool iron if necessary. Fold,
never hang. Store in cedar.[1]

Idea File:

Tips For Feeling Your Best:

Don't wait for the scale to reach that magical
number before you buy truly flattering clothes.

Get a good night's sleep on a consistent
basis. It's best to set a bedtime for yourself. When you are well-rested, you're
mentally alert, possess a more positive attitude,
and your complexion glows.

What you wear underneath has a noticeable
effect on your outer apparel. *Every* woman
should invest in quality undergarments. If
you're married, your husband will enjoy
seeing you undress!

165

PART III:
LAUGH

PUT SOME FUN IN YOUR LIFE!

"A joyful woman makes a joyful home."

-Author unknown

You won't be fulfilled if you live a life of all work and no play. I can remember back in high school when I worked hard all week to get good grades. I looked forward to Friday so I could attend our school football or basketball game. The weekend was reward time for staying focused all week long.

I can't play every weekend, because I may have to work straight through to meet a publishing deadline or fulfill a speaking engagement, but I know that fun is the ultimate gift you can give yourself. So I schedule fun activities and functions. I also engage in having fun spontaneously. For example, my husband and I were in New York walking in Times Square and there were groups of people giving shoulder and neck massages on the streets. I encouraged my husband to stop and get one with me. Ten minutes later we felt refreshed and walked away laughing about how just about anything is possible in New York.

169

My husband and I have learned to put fun in our marriage and family. Once a week we have a date night. Usually it's a Thursday after work. Our entire goal for the evening is to have fun and really enjoy one another's company. Sometimes we go to a movie or drive around and talk. Other times we dine out, visit a bookstore or rent a movie.

I strive to make our home a fun place to live. We laugh a lot at our house. We play games with our children and provide a fun environment for their friends. I believe that when you make time to have fun, you'll get refreshed and it helps you to achieve your goals faster.

Often on the weekend, my husband and I will drive approximately an hour out of town to go to a particular restaurant just for the fun of it. Two of my friends told me about how they went into a designer boutique and tried on very expensive gowns just for the fun of it. They said that several times they had passed by the store and imagined what one of those gowns would look like on. Then one afternoon, they got bold and walked in. Two hours later after trying on several designer originals they thanked the sales lady and told her they'd think about it.

Every year I try to make the going back to school experience fun and exciting for my children. For the past few years, a friend and I have taken our daughters on a back to school shopping trip. We drive to Chicago and spend two full days of shopping for school clothes, eating out at the restaurants of their choice, watching movies, visiting sights, and fellowshipping together. We always stay in a grand hotel so the girls can get the ultimate pampered shopping experience. Now my daughter associates going back to school with fun.

If you're married, have romantic fun. Don't let your intimacy die. The more feminine you feel, the more romantic fun you'll have with your husband. Buy and wear lingerie to bed. Trade ten minute back rubs with your spouse. Use a lightly scented massage oil. Don't get in the rut of making love in the same place, in the same way, at the same time. Do something out of the ordinary. Take short breaks together, check into a nice hotel and spend an entire day being intimate. Send the children away and take advantage of the whole house. Remember, it's legal when you're married.

Idea File:

Ten Tips for "Fun Filled" Living:

ONE: Take a Beauty Retreat.
Spend a whole day with a friend getting
beauty treatments, new hairdos, manicures, pedi-
cures, body massages, make-overs, and top
it off with a new outfit.

TWO: Go to a Professional Game. Hang out
at a football, basketball or baseball game and really cheer for
your team.

THREE: Spend a Day at the Bookstore (preferably one with a cafe). Gather up several books and sip a
cup of tea and relax until you feel like going home.

FOUR: Have a Party. Have your friends over just for
the fun of it. Play games, talk and laugh a lot.

FIVE: Bake. Make their favorite cake or cookies and
then serve them while they are still warm to your friends or
family.

SIX: Travel. Visit a nearby city to shop, sight-see, and dine out. You'll gain new fun experiences.

SEVEN: Play Boardgames
Pick a night and gather your children or friends. Keep a collection of new up to date games around the house. Games are not just for kids.

EIGHT: Surprise your Husband
Purchase a new exotic night gown. Variety adds excitement.

NINE: Read a Children's Book
Sometimes children's books stir up your creativity. They also help you reflect on the simple pleasures in life.

TEN: Find a Hobby
Make time on a regular basis for a craft or an activity you enjoy. For example, scrapbooking, painting, drawing, etc.

DO MORE OF WHAT YOU LOVE

"When you do what you love these activities shouldn't cause you to have an attack of carnality, but instead should refuel you to continue on in the things that God has called you to."

-Stacia Pierce

When we fill our lives with the things that we truly love, life becomes more satisfying to us. Happy people do what they love along with what needs to be done. Women become free when they stop worrying about what people might think and just be themselves. I'm not talking about resisting the necessary changes you need to make, but rather adding the little things that make life so rich and exciting.

Over the last two years I have discovered the things that really bring me joy. For so long, I neglected what was important to me because I felt that it was a waste of time, but when I finally gave into my desire, I actually doubled my time and output. My love for reading has lead me to just loaf in a good bookstore. Spending time in the bookstore is one of my creative outlets. When I come home from a book store, I'm energized and stirred with ideas.

I also love fresh flowers in my house. I use to be hesitant about spending the money for fresh flowers instead of on more groceries. Then I just decided that I was going to fill my house with what I loved. The color, the aroma, the freshness, the beauty and the romance it displays delights me.

I love smoothies and I'm eating one right now, as I write this chapter. I love the taste, as well as the nutritional value. Just about every day, I have a smoothie in my special cup. One of my employees bought me what she called an author's cup and saucer for Christmas, and I started a tradition of eating only my smoothies out of it. I love the smoothies and what the cup represents.

I'm beginning to love exercise. Right now, it's still a task, and I still have resistance toward it, but I love the emotions that go along with exercise. It makes me feel healthy (it should since it is a healthy activity). It makes me feel self-confident, accomplished, and youthful.

I love writing books. I love the research, the layout, the planning of the book, the deadlines, and gathering ideas. I love the tools I use to make the project come to life- the colored pencils, colored index cards, colored dots for reminders, post it tablets and bright colored notebooks. I love sitting in my bed with my scented candle burning, folders all around me and creating chapters that come together to make a book. The finished product is the most rewarding. However, seeing the project completed is a sigh of relief. Then, I love seeing the women who buy the books thumb through the pages and remark "I really need this." I feel like I have accomplished the will of God at that point, because I know the book will change someone's life.

What do you love that you haven't engaged in? What's really important to you? Is your life filled with doing those things that are important to you? These are good journal questions; answer them truthfully in your journal. Then write out some simple solutions to how you will do more of what you love. When you balance what you love to do with what has to be done, you actually become a more productive person. You have to set aside small daily blocks of time for yourself. Use it to sneak in the last few chapters of the book you've been trying to finish, or to play a board game with your family, or simply to relax and dream a little.

Create time retreats. Periodically do something unusual like having a midweek picnic in the park with a friend, visiting a museum, or riding though a really nice neighborhood and look for your dream house.

Rethink your job. Are you doing what you enjoy? Is your current job moving you in the direction of accomplishing your dreams or mission in life? Is it too much stress? Too little satisfaction? Also ask yourself, are you uncomfortable with every job that you do? There may be issues in you that you must deal with. Are you just being lazy? Are your expectations unrealistic?

178

 # Idea File:

Make your life more exciting. Enjoy life more. You can live a great life even while on a budget. Doing what you love doesn't have to be costly. Here is a list of simple ways to enjoy life and incorporate more of what you love. Choose one thing you love, and do it this week.

If you love entertaining:

* Have a dessert party off the cuff.
* Have a spa party with friends.
* Do brunch one Saturday at your house.
* Invite someone over for dinner.
* Host a tea party.
* Have a pot luck.
* Have a book party. Have everyone bring their favorite book for discussion.

If You Love Solitude

* Spend a day in bed reading and writing.

* Go camping.

* Take walks.

* Spend time taking a luxurious bubble bath.

* Take your lunch break alone.

* Tend a garden.

* Get up early in the morning before everyone else. Enjoy the calm before the rest of the house awakes.

* Go to bed early.

* Write letters to family and friends.

* Have a private tea party. Take out your fancy teacup and have a pastry with it.

If You Love Clothes and Fashion

* Have a makeup party.

* Play dress-up with all those outfits and jewelry that have been hiding in your closet and drawers. Experiment with new looks.

* Shop for new underwear.

* Just go shopping.

* Take a mall vacation. Take two days to shop in your favorite malls.

* Buy fashion magazines and cut out your favorite styles.

* Buy books about fashion and makeup.

* Enroll in a fashion design course.

180

If You Love Being Pampered

* Replace worn out bath towels with thick, fluffy new ones.

* Get rid of all faded and mismatched bed sheets. Replace them with colors you love, and matching sets in fabrics that feel good.

* Put fresh flowers in all your bathrooms and bedrooms.

* Buy yourself a foot massage machine and use it often.

* Trade twenty-minute back rubs with your spouse.

* Have breakfast in bed on your bed tray.

* Go to a professional masseuse for a full body massage.

* Get you hair done weekly and get scalp massages.

* Burn scented candles while you read a good book.

* Take a bubble bath with an aromatherapy bath gel. To make the bath more inviting, buy a small inflatable bath pillow.

* Polish your toenails.

If You Love Activity

* Go roller skating.

* Join an aerobics class.

* Try rock climbing.

* Go shopping at the mall.

* Spend a day with your kids and let them set the agenda.

* Go on a date with your husband.

* Travel.

* Workout daily.

181

If You Love Being Creative

* Become a buyer of empty books (journals).

* Buy a fresh box of crayons, colored pencils and sketch pad, and use it as your creativity journal.

* Read your favorite children's book, or find a new children's book to share with your kids.

* Go sight seeing. Visit a new place your haven't seen before; a park, museum, botanical garden, neighborhood etc.

* Read something new and unusual for you.

* Play music.

Now list 25 things you love

In your journal make your own list of 25 things you love to do.

For example;

1. Fresh flowers

2. Shopping

3. New York Cheesecake

4. Reading

5. Flying

6. Scented Candles

7. Bright Colors

8. Decorating

9. Makeup

10. Shoes

182

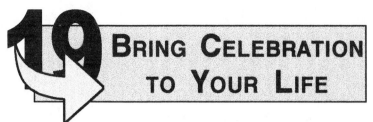

BRING CELEBRATION TO YOUR LIFE

"Those who bring sunshine into the lives of others, cannot keep it from themselves."

-James M. Barrie

One easy, effective and enjoyable way to build a great family heritage and connect with those you love is through bringing celebration into your life. Creating fun family rituals add more meaning to your family time together.

I began to develop some new celebration rituals for each season because I realized my family was just celebrating the holidays in the same fashion in which we were raised. Some traditions were good to keep; others needed to be dismissed. It does take some planning and a little work to make special occasions a very significant and memorable time. However, once you begin practicing unique family rituals, you won't want to have a dull holiday again. Our lives would be boring if we didn't add some excitement and adventure on purpose.

Last year, I went as far as to creating a celebration center. Shelves of party materials like wrapping papers, colored tissue, spools of ribbon, gift bags, boxes, ornaments, glitter, and other supplies decorate  my celebration center in my basement. Then I reserved a drawer to keep my collection of unique paper products including paper plates, cups, matching napkins and table-

 cloths. Having party materials on hand makes it easy to turn any ordinary event into an extraordinary celebration.

Summer Sleepover

I started a fun tradition for my daughter Ariana at the end of every school year. We plan a big summer sleepover in July with all her school and church friends that she does not get the chance to see as frequently during the summer. We usually come up with a theme together and plan a fun filled night of movies, popcorn and pizza.

184

Also in the summer we have loads of fun with our family. We take two vacations- one for the children, and one for my husband and I. We always take on some new adventure. Our family also does a summer reading program. Ariana gets money for every book that she completes. Enjoy the summer by purposing to make it fun.

Winter Tea Time

As soon as the winter season approaches, and we begin to feel the chill and see the frost on the windows, I take a special shopping trip to stock up on herbal tea and hot chocolate. I keep my tea cups visible and the tea kettle on the stove as a reminder to take a tea break.

Our family excitedly anticipates weekend teatime gathering around our kitchen table. We talk, and play board games while sipping our hot, body warming drinks. In Michigan, we have some winter days that are hard to weather. On those days I try to prepare a treat for my children's arrival home from school. As they hit the door, the smell of baked cookies or hot cinnamon rolls greet them and they know we are about to have a special after school tea break.

Don't succumb to the winter blues, but make your home a warm, inviting and uplifting place to be. Seasons come and pass, so take advantage of these times to make a positive impact on your family. Brighten your house by burning potpourri, adding lots of light, placing pretty vases of fresh flowers everywhere and playing soothing worship music. The things that happen in our home and our upbringing define who we are, where we've been and perhaps where we are going. When I started my own family I had to renew my mind to the ways we could bring celebration into our lives. I wanted our family to have "wow experiences and life changing days!" From the time of this writing, the next Women's Success Audio Club message I'm about to do is entitled, "Wow Experiences and Life Changing Days." I believe when we plan for and expect "wow" experiences and life changing days, they will emerge often!

Create Memorable Birthdays

My husband and I want to create memorable, life changing events for our children, so we use their birthdays as an opportunity to do something unique and special for them.
Last year, I hosted an authentic, formal tea

party for my daughter Ariana's eighth birthday. It was beautiful. The girls decorated porcelain tea cups, ate tea cookies and sandwiches. All dressed up for the occasion they looked like little dolls. Ariana and her friends still talk about it to this day. I use birthdays as a way to introduce our children to another meaningful stage in their life. The theme of Ariana's party this year was "Ariana's Success Story." What a special way to introduce her to the importance of personal improvement. My son will be turning two on his next birthday and we'll use his party to celebrate with him what he loves...basketball.

What To Do To Create Memories

① Go all out with decorations. Ambiance does matter. Decorating creates an atmosphere.

② Take lots of pictures.
Capture those sacred moments on film.

③ Put your photos in a scrap book.
Write a brief story, description or witty comment about

the event next to your pictures.

4 Video tape your Event.

You can reminisce and watch your own home videos later.

5 Create memorable themes for each of your celebrations.

My husband and I have made it a part of our family mission to enjoy life together. On purpose, we bring celebration into our lives. For instance, for Valentines Day this year my husband was creative. Instead of bringing home flowers, candy, a card and going out to dinner, he gave me a shopping budget and an entire day with him at the mall of my choice. Needless to say I had a great time. I spent most of the money on makeup and perfume.

I put a lot of work into my May women's conference to make it a "wow" experience and life changing days. I am convinced that information changes the seasons of our lives. One idea can put your life in motion toward a new direction. Atmosphere, meaning, color, sounds, and attitudes also help to create a wow experience. So for the conference I plan how we will decorate in detail. All of my speakers and I saturate ourselves in the word, prayer, and really study our subjects to ensure women's lives are changed.

188

For the next event you host, put a lot of thought into it. Keep this question before you: "How can I put celebration into the lives of others. When you take the time to add celebration to your life and to those you love, you break up the monotony of life. Create a celebration budget. It's good to always have money to reward yourself for being disciplined. Plan for spontaneous fun by transforming your ordinary mealtime into a special occasion. Dress the dinner table. Complete it with a centerpiece and candles and have a positive topic for discussion ready.

Every now and then, go all out with a "big deal" occasion complete with invitations, elaborate decorations and lavish foods. Also add in those "just for fun" celebrations. I'm in the midst of planning one now for Easter with my daughter. I'm hosting a Young Author's Party for her. Each girl will get a blank hard cover book to fill with an exciting story of their personal victories and design a beautiful cover. We'll all have tea, scones and lots of fun.

This year decide to add more celebration to your life; it doesn't take much really, just a little creative thought.

Idea File:

*Plan a celebration and make it a big deal. The whole process will stretch your mind and cause you to grow!

*Get my tape "How to Celebrate the Seasons" to get ideas for Halloween, Thanksgiving, Christmas and more.

MAINTAIN LASTING FRIENDSHIPS

"I can trust my friends. These people force me to examine, encourage me to grow."

-Cher.

The right friends are essential to your success in life. Who you associate with affects your beliefs, attitude and outlook. Proverbs 29:19 (TLB) tells us; "A mirror reflects a man's face, but what he is really is, is shown by the kind of friends he chooses." First, you must evaluate your closest relationships and see if they are making a positive impact on your life. If necessary, begin to change your close associations. You should be able to trust your friends. They should force you to examine yourself and encourage you to grow. Experts now have concrete evidence that friendships actually boost your immune system, improve the quality of your life and help you live longer.

Make a list of your five closet friends. Now estimate the annual income of each. Total them and divide by five. Your income will probably fall somewhere in the middle of these five. If you want to go to another level, you might consider making new friends with those who are living the life you want. You'll find that you'll raise your standard of living to meet theirs. You can't be afraid to have friends that stretch you. Their lives and expectations should stretch you. These are healthy relationships.

If you don't have a team of good friends, the Bible gives the instruction to first be friendly yourself. Over the years I have acquired a great assortment of friends who are gifted in different ways. In some of my friendships we talk to each other at least once a month. Others we may only verbally communicate once a year. However, I try to keep those closest to me updated on what's happening in my life and vice versa.

> *"True friendship is like sound health, the value of it is seldom known until it be lost."*
> *-Colton*

Most women are so incredibly busy that it's difficult to find the time and energy to show our best buddies that we care. But good friends invent ways to keep in touch and nurture each other. We can keep our lives so busy that we close the door to divine encounters while we are pursuing our life's mission. We also have to be balanced, so that we don't build barriers that reduce opportunities for true friendship.

"Good Friends Invent Ways to Nurture Each Other and Keep in Touch."

The following strategies are principles that I learned, practice and share with other women to help them build strong lasting friendships.

20 Sure Fire Ways to Build Lasting Friendships!

1 Remember to be Grateful

Practice your appreciation of a friend's kindness, whether it's an invitation to dinner, a favor, or a gift. Say thank you right away by phone or note. Never take their gestures for granted.

2 Share Your Dreams

A good friend should know where you are headed in life and share your same enthusiasm about your future. All of your friends won't be "dream mates," but share your plans with the ones who are. Share your dreams with friends who think big. I have a few friends with which I can share the projects I'm working on, and my plans for the future. They get just as excited as I am about it.

3 Be Affectionate

Give plenty of hugs, especially when saying hello or good-bye. Embrace your friends when you hear good or bad news from them. This shows that you truly care about the relationship.

4 Be An Encourager

Encourage your friends in their goals and dreams. Give them praise when they achieve something they've been striving for. Be a carrier of good news and always have an up-lifting conversation with friends.

5 Don't Over Look Special Days

Keep a stash of cards on hand to send out for birthdays, anniversaries, and other special occasions. Remember your friends at Christmas and New Years. Cards are an easy way to keep up with friends and show that you are thinking about them.

6 Give Good Gifts

I love to give, so it is really easy for me to find good gifts for my friends. Most of my friends live in another city or state so we don't see each other frequently, which is why I try to always take a gift that I know they would love. Make investments in your friends.

7 Laugh Together

Laughing together creates a bonding effect. You cherish those good times you have in your life. When I get together with my friends, we plan to have fun. We aren't stiff or rigid around one another, but instead we do fun activities together or engage in meaningful yet exciting conversations.

8 Plan Inspiring Outings

My husband and I invited our friends from Ohio to meet us in

Manhattan, New York for three days of adventure. We flew in separately and met up at the same hotel. We had a riot, going to a Broadway production, seeing a 3-D movie, walking down the streets of New York at midnight, dining out, riding in a limousine, and laughing the entire trip. Special times of bonding with your friends are never forgotten.

9. Forgive and Forget

Friends, just like siblings, will have misunderstandings and spats. But if you know the person is supposed to be a part of your life and is connected to your destiny, then fight to keep the relationship in good standing. Say you're sorry if you have done something offensive.

10. Never Criticize Her Husband

If your friend is married and has a "falling- out" with her husband, never get in agreement with her negativity about her mate. Always encourage her to do what is right, and don't give your personal opinions. Instead, give advice and counsel based on the word of God.

11. Show Pride in her Children

I always ask about my friends' children and send my love to them.

Remember your friendship goes beyond just the two of you.

You must be concerned about what's in her world. If you hear a noteworthy accomplishment of a friends' child, then congratulate her and share in her happiness. If you plan on seeing the whole family, take gifts for the kids.

12 Be a Good Listener

Don't monopolize the whole conversation, but bring attention to their needs and concerns. James 1:19 says, "Let every woman be quick to hear and slow to speak." Listening means setting aside whatever is going on in your life and giving your full attention to them.

13 Pray for Her

Include them in your daily prayer. Also, whenever you find out that they are believing God for a breakthrough in an area, or have a need, get in agreement. Add them to your prayer list and confess the Word of God over their situation. For example, some of our friends are involved in building projects. So are we, but we also pray for their buildings to be completed or purchased, as well.

14 Collect Informative Information

Whenever you see books, articles, tips or any information that will help further your friends' purpose, get it and give it. Sow into your friends' lives and you will surely reap a harvest of rewards. Give your friends idea strategies. If you see something that will cause their creativity to soar, give it to them. I bought my friend a calendar that was in line with her purpose. I knew it would spark ideas for her ministry to soar.

15 Be Open and Honest

Be truthful about your feelings, but respectful. Friends will not always agree on every issue, but that is no reason to cancel the friendship. Once I had to tell a friend the truth about her attitude. At first she was a little upset, but soon she admitted that she was constantly displaying a negative attitude. When she changed, her life changed.

16 Don't Compete

Quite possibly, you and your friend may be in different seasons in your life, spiritually, naturally, mentally and financially. So never compare yourself to your friends' accomplishments. If they are ahead of you in an area, gleam from them, learn and give them praise. If your friend isn't quite where you are in an area, offer support, insight, and encouragement for them to continue to grow! Good friends respect and honor one another!

17 Help Her Progress

As I move through life, I set aside good ideas and proven formulas to encourage and inspire my friends. If you have a friend who is facing a problem or road block to her success in life, share any winning formulas you may have.

18 Keep God at the Center of Your Relationship

Talk about God to one another. Pray together if a difficult situation arises. Discuss what God has placed on your heart.

19 Stay Flexible

Though most friendships are built around similar interests and temperaments, they are maintained by tolerating differences. Learn to respect the different choices your friends may make, as long as they are sound biblical choices. Accept the different seasons in each others life and you will be able to remain good friends. Be sure to allow your friends room to grow and to change.

20 Have a Determined Commitment

True friendship requires work. It takes time to mature the relationship. You need to talk and share with each other.

To be a good friend you have to be willing to work through misunderstandings. Learn to survive differences of opinion and agree to disagree.

Idea File:

* Make new extraordinary associations
* Get to know some new people this week
* Write a letter to a friend
* Don't try to force a friendship that doesn't seem to be clicking.

*Meet a friend for breakfast. Talk honestly about your lives, your passions and pursuits.

* Take a trip with a close friend, go away for a couple of days to a nice hotel and share, read, shop, laugh and dine out. Just do what you love.

GIVE YOUR GUESTS THE ROYAL TREATMENT

"The happiest people are those who do the most for other people."

-Booker T. Washington

Whether you are hosting guests in your home or you are residing over a big event, the way that you treat your guests will greatly determine the outcome of your time spent together. Always keep in mind that your guests have taken out precious time to spend with you. Being a traveling speaker, I experience at times some aggravating situations.

Recently, I was asked to speak for fifteen to twenty minutes on the topic of "Successful Entrepreneurship in the 90's" at a conference (where there was supposed to be 700 people in attendance). I was told that my presentation was scheduled for 6:30pm, and to arrive one hour early. I arrived promptly at 5:30pm to find myself one of the first people there. I searched around for the host or someone who could direct me, when I finally discovered that I had walked past the host several times. I enthusiastically walked up to him to introduce myself and see where he wanted me to go.

The host's reply was that he was too busy now, "Just go in the conference room and find a table to set up your stuff." and he brisked off. I thought, "This must get better." So my attendants and I set up my books and tapes and found ourselves a seat. Around 7:30p.m., I finally asked the host again when we were planning to get started and whether or not a cordless mike and podium were available. He said, "No neither are available." Unless I stood

The host's reply was that he was too busy then, "Just go in the conference room and find a table to set up your stuff."

in the far corner and did my speech (that was where the podium was plugged in). You can just imagine how the night ended up.

I was finally summoned to the stage (from the back of the room since there was no reserved seating for me) at 8:30pm. On my way up the stairs he told me, "Please remember to keep it to 15 minutes. We're trying to keep things on schedule." I laughed and went and grabbed one of the musicians microphones. I talked for 15 minutes, the audience applauded my message, then I left the stage. As the event came to a close at 10:00pm, I went to talk to the host. I respectfully explained to him that he wasn't going to go far if he treated all of his guests this way.

That's just one of my stretching experiences. The only other one that tops that is when I was the guest speaker at an event and asked to pay a table fee to display my books and tapes, along with the registration fee for my two assistants that travel with me. The fees that our ministry paid to the host were more than the honorarium I received from them for speaking. I just chalked it up as experience, believing that they couldn't have possibly known better. I also knew I would never return to that location or recommend it to any of my colleagues.

The way you treat people will affect your relationship with them. Our ministry hosts several events every year and it is a mandate for our entire staff and volunteer staff to treat our guests with the utmost respect. We have a royal treatment policy and procedures to ensure that we practice consistency with any guest speaker that speaks at our church.

Before our guest ever arrives we find out all of our their likes and dislikes from food to color choices.

If you are hosting an event never put your guests into someone's home unless they request it, or you've discussed it with them previously and they have agreed to it. Always give your guest the option of being in a nice hotel, preferably a five-star hotel. Whether you have house guests or a guest for a professional event, gifts in their room always adds a welcoming touch. Snacks make it convenient for your guest so they don't have to go to the gift shop or find a nearby store. We make sure our guests always have a refrigerator in the room to keep their water and juices cold. The more you sow into your guest the more you will reap. Hospitality is all about giving.

Good communication also helps make the stay less stressful. If guests are staying in your home, communicate with them what bathroom they can use, where the coffee pot is, and that they can help themselves if they get up before you do. We had a couple come stay with us for a few days just for fun and fellowship. I put a welcome basket in their room with toothpaste, toothbrushes, body lotion for her and shaving cream for him. I also included a few gift books, some homemade goodies, and placed fresh flowers on the night stand in their room. After they left, my friend wrote me a beautiful letter expressing her thankfulness for the royal treatment. She felt truly pampered and welcomed.

Communication With Your Guest Speaker

Your guest speaker should never be wondering what's going to happen next. Type out in detail what the schedule and plans are for your event. Then your speaker will know how to stay on track with you. For example, if you plan to take them to dinner or lunch after they speak, let them know, but always give them the option to retire to their room if they are fatigued. If you're traveling and speaking all the time, you just want some rest and solitude after speaking, to recuperate. As the host, give your speaker a phone number or contact person to get in touch with you if necessary.

V.I.P.S.

If you are hosting an event and some VIP's (very important people) show up in addition to your guest of honor, be sure to give them some sort of general recognition for supporting you. It's just good manners.

Give Honor Where Honor is Due

You give honor to a guest speaker by giving them an excellent introduction. But the main way you give honor, is to pay them well for their input. If you have no idea what to pay a speaker ask someone who has hosted a speaker before. Ask the speaker to give you a ball-park figure of what others have given them. Then try to come close, or better yet, supercede what they normally get.

Highlight Your Special Guest

Often we host conferences with multiple guest speakers. On the night that they speak we ask them to share about the materials that they've brought with them. If a speaker has truly shared life changing information, then you'll probably get tons more when you purchase their books and tapes. When you're hosting, encourage the audience to check out the speakers materials at the tables and grab some take-home goodies.

How to be a Good House Guest

On a few occasions my husband and I have had the privilege of being the house guest of some of our very special friends. Whenever we visit anyone, we adhere to some unwritten rules that makes our stay enjoyable for both parties.

1. Arrive on Time with A Gift in Hand.

A gift displays your gratitude for the host welcoming you into their home. A simple bouquet of flowers is special.

2. Pack Respectfully. Find out ahead of time what your visit entails. What kind of clothes are needed? Will you be attending a black tie dinner? Will you need a swim suit?

3. Your Host Is Not Your Maid. Be ready to put away your own clothes in a neat fashionable way.

4. If you have special dietary needs tell your host before you arrive. Chances are they will have already shopped for groceries before you arrive and this will help them be prepared in advance for you.

5. Clean up After Yourself.

If you take a bath, clean the tub. Keep the sink and counter tops clean as well. Be willing to put your dish in the dishwasher or your plate in the sink.

6. Trash Etiquette. Ask your host how and where she would like you to dispose of any sanitary items if you are visiting during your menstrual cycle.

207

7. Dress Appropriately. Wear modest night apparel. Be comfortable, but covered. Always pack a night gown and slippers.

8. Don't Over Extend Your Stay. Unless your friend has asked you to stay over. Don't wear out your welcome.

9. Keep Your Attitude in Check. Don't be moody, complain, or be pushy about having your way. Go along with the flow of your host and you will have a pleasant stay.

10. Say Thank You. Send a thank you note within a week after your departure and express, in detail, how enjoyable your stay was.

Idea File:

In Proverbs 18:16 it states that; "A man's gift maketh room for him, and bringeth him before great men." The next time you host an event and invite a guest speaker, attend an event, or have house guests, give a gift to them from your heart and watch it make room for you.

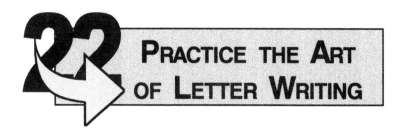

PRACTICE THE ART OF LETTER WRITING

"A short, timely letter can enhance moments of your day... it can be a gem given or received."
-Alexandra Stoddard

Writing or receiving a wonderful letters remains one of the most satisfying means of communicating with other people. Writing letters is a life enhancer. It improves both the writer's and the receiver's life. A letter gives us time to reflect and say more clearly and completely what we wish to say. After teaching on letter writing to the women in my church, their relationships with family and friends improved.

Letter writing has been described as a lost art. I believe one of the reasons women don't engage in letter writing that often, is because it is time consuming. I'm a very busy person myself, but I made writing letters to certain people a priority. Consequently, I put time into my schedule to write letters. This past summer, I traveled across the country on a

209

book signing tour for my last book, *25 Ways Women Can Motivate Themselves*. While in Dallas the thought came to me to write my husband a love letter. I hadn't done that since we were newlyweds, so I bought a really nice card and wrote my husband a very passionate love note. I expressed to him how I appreciated his support of my dreams. Not only was he very anxious for me to get home, but he also appreciated me saying thanks.

Usually the morning that I leave for a trip, I put a letter in my daughter's lunch box that expresses my love for her and encourages her. While I'm away I write a letter to both of my children and tell them about my trip.

Letters have to be a powerful vehicle, of communication because companies spend thousands of dollars to send direct mail pieces to their customers. I wrote a letter that every woman who joins our ministry receives. The letter simply tells them a little bit about who I am. Then it goes on to explain my vision for women's ministry and how I need their support to cause the vision to unfold. As a result of this letter reaching all the women who join our church, I have great support. The women come out to Bible study and the women's conference. Plus, every week the women's ministry keeps growing. I love to receive letters. For me there is nothing more rejuvenating than to have a cup of tea and sit in bed, or take a bath while reading letters. Weekly I receive letters from readers about my book or from women who heard me speak. I read each letter. These letters are so encouraging, because they let me know that what I'm saying and writing about is truly improving women's lives. I often share some of the inspirational testimonies from the letters I receive, and it often encourages others who are facing similar circumstances.

10 Steps to Easy Letter Writing!

1. Be Prepared

Develop your stationery wardrobe which can consist of a number of different styles of paper. Keep fun personalized stationery in a handy spot. I use a bright yellow fabric colored box. It sits on my kitchen counter for easy access. Colorful or decorated paper that fits your personal style makes letter writing more exciting . The stationery you choose makes a statement about you. When I was in New York this summer, I visited a few very unique paper emporiums and bought paper that expresses my retro style.

Keep stamps and envelopes handy. Purchase return address labels. Collect cards for all occasions and keep them on hand. Try to always personalize the card with your own thoughts as well.

2. Create a Letter Writing Day

My daughter and I have one day a month when we write personal letters for about an hour. We look forward to the time together and to sharing what's happening in our lives. Take advantage of "down time," like the time spent sitting in the doctor's or dentist office. It is also a good idea to keep your stationery with you. Make a list of the people you want to write. Remember that even the busiest of successful people find time to communicate in writing.

3. Be Informative

If it's a personal letter tell your friend or relatives about a good book you read or some exciting things that happened on your vacation. I usually try to give some insightful information that will help them fulfill their purpose.

4. Stay Focused

Write as though you were sitting across the table from the person you are writing to. Say what you would say in person.

Keep the same train of thought throughout your letter. But don't conform to any set rules of letter writing. Be yourself!

5. Develop Your Style
I try to make my letters give the readers energy, inspiration, and ideas. I write to motivate and stimulate. What's your style of writing? Are you poetic, humorous, or a romantic writer?

6. Be Inquisitive
By asking questions, you will give the other person something to get started with when they write back to you. Make the questions specific. Ask the "W" questions: Who, What, Where, When and Why.

7. Be Appropriate
When I'm writing letters to my mentors I usually thank them for their impartation and tell them how their information has helped me. I don't expect them to write back. I carefully choose my words when I'm writing a business, or mass mailing letter. You don't want to be interpreted in the wrong way. Reread your letters and possibly have someone else proof read them.

213

8. Express Your Feelings

Write from your heart and learn how to convey what you are feeling with word pictures. A good letter doesn't have to be long. Just pack it with meaningful information. For the best results, write in the right atmosphere, during a time of quiet. Add a vase of flowers to the table before writing. Reflect on beauty and allow your feelings to flow onto the paper.

9. Collect Information

The next time you come across an amusing cartoon, an article in a magazine, a news clipping or read a good book, collect the information and send it to the friend you know has interest in that information. Never throw out a good letter. Start a letter file box.

10. End the Letter on a Positive Note

Don't write depressing, faithless, letters. Write letters of hope, faith and encouragement and your readers will always welcome your letters. Remember to put the day, month and year on your letters or cards; it adds to their value.

214

 **The Benefits of Letter Writing**

1. It helps you to develop your writing style.
2. It makes a more intimate connection. Letters mingle your soul.
3. You can fill someone else's day with joy.
4. It helps you maintain friendships.
5. It exercises your mind and imagination.
6. Letter writing is a restoring way to spend time alone.

 # Idea File:

* Write a note inside each book you give as gifts.

* Buy special letter writing pens.

* Write letters to authors, speakers and mentors who have touched your life. Tell them how they have impacted you.

* Go card and stationary shopping. Now you can go with and new outlook and intent. Your purpose now is to build a collection of cards and papers that express your signature style. Store up so letter writing isn't a task but a treat.

* If you already have tons of stationary and cards, great! Use them. Pull out something fancy and write a colorful letter to a friend you haven't talked with in a while.

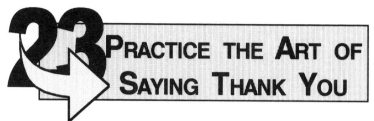

23 PRACTICE THE ART OF SAYING THANK YOU

"The deepest principle in human nature is the craving to be appreciated."

-William James

A verbal thank you is sufficient for most everyday favors, such as borrowing an egg from a neighbor or asking a friend to pick you up for an event that you both plan to attend. Then there are other times when you should show your appreciation by writing a brief letter or a sending a thank you card. Whenever a gift is given to you a written thank you is in order. It's simply good old fashion manners to express your appreciation for the gift you received.

Within the first few months of the release of my book, *25 Ways Women Can Motivate Themselves*, I mailed over 100 gift copies to friends, relatives, mentors and people who have made a positive impact on my life. I was disappointed when only about ten people acknowledged that they received the book and sent thank you letters. I wasn't looking for praise, but I did think most of these people would say thank you.

Since my childhood, my mother has always instilled in us that we should show gratitude when another person has been thoughtful enough to give us a gift. I have been practicing the principle of saying a sincere thank you for a long time. Extraordinary women realize that saying thank you denotes appreciation.

The women who did write to say thanks for the book were the busiest of all the women. These women live exceptional lives full of purpose. Perhaps these women have learned a valuable lesson about saying thank you which has caused them to rise above average to success.

One of the thank you letters came from a lady that I most admire; Jinger Heath, President of Beauty Control Cosmetics. It was her company's mentorship and training that exposed me to some of the greatest motivational speakers of our time. She played a significant role in the shaping of my ministry. I sent Jinger an autographed copy of my book and a letter of appreciation for her impartation into my life. A few weeks later she wrote back a warm thank you letter.

Writing a thank you letter is such an effective way to communicate gratitude to someone who has made a positive impact in your life. Zig Ziglar says, "When you help enough people get what they want, you'll never have lack for what you want." My mission in life is to help ordinary women live out extraordinary lives. Because of the kind thank you letters I receive, I know that I'm hitting the target. I always encourage women when I speak, to send thank you letters to mentors, bosses, pastors, teachers, ministry gifts and conference hosts or hostesses who have imparted into their lives.

Thank-yous and encouraging words have a motivating force behind them which cause people to be strengthened and continue on. I'm going to share 3 letters out of several hundred that I received after my Women's Success conference. All the letters I received touched my heart, but these three in particular were written exceptionally well and are full of heart felt gratitude.

Letter #1
This year's Women's Success Conference was the best women's conference I've ever attended. I've been home for a couple weeks now and I'm still talking about it! There is no way you can put a dollar amount on what I've learned. It's

219

priceless wisdom and revelation of the Word that was shared throughout the conference. It's amazing how each vessel God used to minister the Word had a thorough comprehension of the Word, but also shared the application needed to apply the word in my life. I'm ready to go to a new level and God has prepared me. He has used the Women's Conference to show me how networking, image, dreams, and financing are all in his perfect plan for me! Now I'm equipped, and it feels good. Pastor Stacia you said in three weeks things would change and I want to share with you some changes that have taken place in my life since returning home. First of all, I was elected Vice Chairperson of staff council at my place of employment. Second, I asked my director for a month off work to spend time with my daughter. He said, "That's no problem, August is a good month to be off." Oh, by the way, I'm a single mother and every bill will still be paid on time or ahead of time even with the month off work.

God is faithful to his word, Philippians. 4:19. Third, I plan to pursue my studies in ministry. I'm so excited I can't wait to see what's in store for the 1999 Women's Success Conference! I'll be praying for you and the LCCC family, please pray for me!
Sincerely,
Charisse

Letter #2

Dear Stacia;

Conference Host

The conference was wonderful! I have a fourteen year old daughter that I brought along with me. We thoroughly enjoyed the conference. Excellence was reflected in every aspect of the conference. I learned something in every session that I sat in. Financial, Success Talk, the Teen Summit etc. Thanks so much for bringing this to Lansing. It will make a difference in mine and my daughter's lives.

Mary

Letter #3

Dear Pastor Stacia;

I would like to express my heartfelt gratitude toward you, Pastor James and the Women's Leadership Team for opening your hearts and pouring your lives into us. When Minister Daphine said that our purpose was not for ourselves but for others, it gave me such a revelation about the significance of fulfilling our purpose. It also gave me a greater appreciation for you and Pastor James. If you had not obeyed the call on your lives, thousands of lives would be lost.

When Minister Dena spoke about "Success Talk," it caused me to reflect upon the (word seeds) that you have sown into my life.

221

The Holy Spirit brought to my remembrance words that you had sown into my life and showed me how much they meant to me and affected my life. Back in February of 1996 you prophesied to me at a Women in the Word meeting. You said things to me that only the Holy Spirit knew. I was hurting so bad that day, I was depressed, I felt so defeated and wanted to give up. As you prophesied to me you said three words that totally changed the way I saw myself, you called me a woman of God, and like Gideon, I did not see myself the way God sees me.

Those (word seeds) you sowed began to take root in my life. Your encouraging words and compliments have motivated me and brought to life my God-given gifts. I have been in the process of creating an entire new wardrobe because of your words of kindness and encouragement. I could go on and on about the wonderful speakers and the many ways you and Pastor James have impacted my life over the past 3 1/2 years, but because I value your time as well as my own, I will try to keep this to a minimum (you taught me that too ~smile~).

You have caused me to dream and to believe in myself for the first time in my adult life. Because of your words and teachings, I am in the process of starting a catering business. Because of you, Pastor James and the Life Changers Family, I have hope and am excited about life. Because of you I believe I can have a successful life.

I thank God for you and what He is doing through you. (I'm crying again) smile.

I love you all so very much,
Anna

dea File:

Reflect for a moment have you forgotten to say thank you to someone who has helped you, inspired you, stretched you or believed in you? What about your husband, children or closest friend? When is the last time you wrote them a letter to say thanks? Make a note of all the people you want to write thank you letters to over the next thirty days.

24 FRAME YOUR FUTURE

"Don't let the future be held hostage by the past."
-Neil Maxwell

Every great dream begins with the end in mind. When you frame your dreams with faith photos it helps you to clarify the dream. A picture gives you something to target and focus on.

I developed the Prayer and Purpose Planner to act as a personal dream book in which a dreamer places pictures or images from magazines, newspapers or photos to represent their dreams. Included in my Prayer and Purpose planner are book covers of future books I'll write, beautiful homes, places I want to visit, photos of my family having fun together, romantic pictures of married couples on vacation and dining out, church buildings and much more. The pictures in my planner represent a goal. Pictures provide stimulation for dreaming.

Women all over the country are ordering my Prayer and Purpose Planner and are testifying of their phenomenal results. Last year at my Women's Success Conference, I had a Prayer

225

and Purpose Planner Party. I had hundreds of assorted magazines, brochures, and news clippings spread out across the platform along with glue sticks, scissors and tape in baskets to equip the women to create. They were encouraged to browse through the magazines and find pictures that represent their dreams and begin to paste them

in the appropriate places in their planner. The atmosphere was electric. Hundreds of women were discussing their future and how they would go about accomplishing their dreams.

A few months after the conference, I began to get letters from women across the country saying how many of their dreams were already beginning to manifest. Taking a few minutes every day to look through your Prayer and Purpose Planner will cause you to seize and secure your dreams because your mind will be motivated and your spirit inspired. Soon, ideas and strategies on how to cause your dreams to come to pass will flood your mind. Your faith photos act like magnets. When coupled with prayer and positive, faith-filled confessions, you have winning solutions to realizing your dreams. God used the principle of visualization throughout the Bible to cause men and women of God to succeed.

226

Hebrews 11:3 describes the process: *"Through faith we understand that the worlds were framed by the word of God, so that things which are seen were not made of things which do appear."* Joshua 1:8 tells us; *"This book of the law shall not depart out of thy mouth; but thou shall meditate therein day and night, that thou mayest observe to do according to all that is written therein: for then thou shalt make thy way prosperous, and then thou shalt have good success."* Usually, before retiring to bed, I take a few moments to look through my dream book. My mind becomes motivated and often ideas or strategies on how to make my dreams come to pass will emerge.

Every time I work on a new book, I begin with a mock cover design which I keep a copy at my desk and also in my Prayer and Purpose Planner. The book cover motivates me to complete the project. The great achievers of our day have framed their future by first imagining their success before they actually obtained it. The future belongs to those who believe in the beauty of their dreams. Aristotle Onassis said that he saw his first ship in his mind before he acquired it.

Carl Lewis told reporters he visualized that he would match Jesse Owens historic record at the Olympics. He got exactly what he visualized, he only matched Owens record; he didn't break it.

Creflo Dollar visualized the World Dome, and now he is in it and the building is paid for in full. Dr. I.V. Hilliard said when other ministries would mock him about having a large T.V. ministry, a large congregation and a quality lifestyle, he would spend time daily in godly meditation visualizing himself already achieving his dreams. Now he has all of them! A few years back we were in an auditorium that we weren't filling up. My husband had the ushers begin to put out chairs to fill the room. Every week we would turn and wave to the empty chairs, believing that there would soon be people to fill them. We visualized the room full and got photos of other churches with full services like our Pastor, Bishop Keith A. Butler of Word of Faith International. Within months, the place began to fill up. Now we have three services on Sundays and have moved to a bigger location with well over a thousand members.

Proverbs 23:7 says "As a man thinketh, so is he." Begin to think and focus in the direction of your dreams. When you begin to frame your future you give your life direction. It has been said that "When you don't know where you're headed, any road will lead you there." Head in the direction of your dreams. Gather your own dream building photos and put them in your prayer and purpose planner. You are moved, motivated and triggered by sight, so you need visual models to support your goals.

Next, frame your future with words. Written out prayers and faith confessions activate your dreams. The Bible tells us that death and life are in the power of the tongue. You have to be careful to speak life bearing words over yourself and your dreams. Whenever you speak the word of God over your dreams you are breathing life into them. In my Prayer and Purpose Planner, I have written out several prayers for my children's purpose, health, schooling and protection. I have written confessions for my husband and our purpose, health, protection, church members etc. Written confessions help you to target your faith.

Idea File:

A System for Framing your Future:

1. Create a dream page: Look over your dream list and pick five things you want to focus on in the next six months. Now transfer that information into your Prayer & Purpose Planner

2. Empower your Dreams with Faith Photos: Collect pictures from magazines, catalogs and brochures that will give you a visual model of your goals. For instance, if you're working on losing weight, find a picture of a body you admire and glue your face on it. If you want new clothes, and a certain appearance, find the outfits and glue your face on them in your planner. Now visualize yourself looking fabulous. You have just framed your future.

Frame your Future with YOUR WORDS!

3. Energize your Pictures with Words:

Write out all your faith confessions or cut out words and phrases from magazines that support your dreams.

4. Get your Dreams in Order

Frame your pictures and words in a categorized way in your prayer and purpose planner. For convenience, my planner has already been categorized for you.

5. Look at Your Planner Consistently

Look at your planner often - daily if possible. This form of godly meditation will allow the Holy Spirit to give you ideas, insight and the "know how" to make your dreams come true.

6. Order a Prayer & Purpose Planner Today

To order call: 1-517-333-9860 Cost: only $39.95

You have a responsibility to frame your future and live out your purpose. Whether you want to believe it or not,

"You owe somebody!" There are people who need you to fulfill your purpose so they can accomplish theirs. Plus, despite the fact you may have had some negative experiences in your life, there are people who have sown into you and you owe it to them to live an extraordinary life. Ultimately you owe it to God to fulfill his will for your life.

25 ABSORB LIFE

"Keep your eyes on the roam."

-Stacia Pierce

When you absorb life you become aware of your surroundings. It wasn't until I began to absorb life that I began to live a extraordinary life. It's amazing how we can go through life and be so shallow and not even know it. It's not until you come in contact with extraordinary people that you realize life is full of pleasure.

When you began to absorb life, everyday is a fun adventure; life becomes invigorating and refined. A simple trip to the grocery store no longer is a task, but a treat. In order to absorb life to its fullest you must read more, listen attentively and get out more. Visit people and places that share your passions. Attend women's conferences that are in line with your convictions. Roam the malls. Do lunch at an exquisite restaurant.

Become an Idea Collector

Do your homework, it will put you at the top of the class. For years I have been a researcher, a clipper, a note taker, a file keeper and an advertisement collector. I enjoy the search for ideas. Since my teen years I have had a passion for helping women become their best. I have collected and kept information for years. I get ideas from catalogs, books, magazines, vacation sites, malls and home interiors.

Last week I bought a book that cost me sixteen dollars, and I didn't buy it to read. When I saw the cover and the colors, immediately it gave me ideas for a project that I was working on. I placed the book on my desk at the office for inspiration. I have several files full of women's ministry ideas I've collected over the years. Right now I'm acting on some of the ideas that I collected over five years ago.

To collect ideas begin with observing. But don't stop there. You must read, clip, visit, take notes, keep files and then take action with your ideas. Get creative with your files and it will be more inviting to keep up with them. Paint a file cabinet your favorite color, use a creative file box, use brightly colored filing folders. This will invite you to play.

Absorb Books

I love how Peter Cornrall states; "Your books are your personal history. You are what you read." Being extraordinary in life is the result of being well rounded and well read. Build an extraordinary library of books that surround your purpose. Read with pen and paper nearby so you can capture an outstanding quote, write down an intriguing idea, or put a note on your "To Do" list. So much of life's flavor can be found in books.

Earn a Masters Degree in Details

When you walk into a beautiful room that is breathtaking and you really enjoy the atmosphere, look around. What makes that room so beautiful to you? Is it the colors, lights, furniture, or arrangements? Notice the details. Once you get tuned into your purpose you'll being to notice all sorts of resources and ideas that you can use. You will zoom in on those objects, information or people that consume your thought life and edit out other things that aren't important to you at the time.

Educate Your Eye to Absorb Life

A few days ago, at the time of this writing, I was in the mall with one of the ladies who helps me coordinate my May Conference fashion show. We walked past a boutique.

and the window display caught my eye. The colors were exactly what I'm using in May. So we went in to inquire about the window dressing. The information I was given gave me some incredible ideas.

 As we go through life, we have to take the blinders off and raise our heads up so we can see all the beauty and events that surrounds us. Get X-ray vision. Look beyond the surface. There is so much excitement everywhere. I discover fascinating examples everyday for my books, speaking engagements, and women's conferences from many sources.

Set up a Creativity Corner
Every woman needs a personal space- a place to create and dream. Your creativity corner should be filled with things you love. Things that both stimulate you as well as bring you joy. I recently read an article about four female artists, who made dolls, wall hangings, story book characters, and jewelry. The article showed all of their work spaces.

236

When interviewed each of the ladies said they started out with just setting up a place in their home to work on their hobbies, what they loved to do. Eventually it blossomed into a full-time career. Who knows what could become of your creative corner!

My creative corner looks like a kids play station. I'm motivated by color, so my space is filled with colored markers, post-it tabs, pencils, crayons and notebooks. My space invites me to write. I have a tape I did called A Woman's Personal Space. I encourage you to order it. The cassette is life changing and it goes into detail on your creative place and what to fill your personal space with.

Capture the Day

Now that you have become curious about your surroundings, you need to put all the information you gathered into a journal. Journal about your observations, your ideas, and your feelings each day. There is such value in recording what impresses you. It helps you to fine tune your purpose and create your own unique niche.

237

Know your Niche

One day while journalizing I wrote, "Why my obsession with art and decorating? Why do I spend so much on these books? I'm not an artist or an interior decorator, though I love upgrading my surroundings, I'm intrigued by bringing improvement to an environment. I love adding color to that which is dull." Then I mediated a while on my thoughts and then I heard in my spirit,

"Yes, you are an artist; you decorate women's lives." WOW!

That simple phrase from the Lord added a whole new dimension to my purpose and call. While enjoying the hunt for those things that reflect my purpose. The Lord was really refining my mission.

238

Idea File:

Gather pictures and draw illustrations of the things that interest you.

* Take a trip to a place that in some way reflects your passion.

* Decide that you will no longer merely go through life, but you will absorb life and make an impact on your generation.

In Closing

I encourage you to find your course to living an extraordinary life. Know this: no two people are alike . Your road to fulfilling your destiny is uniquely designed. Be yourself. Don't strive to be exactly like anyone else. Remember, if there's two of you, one of you is uneccessary.

Apply each one of these easy principles to your life and in time you will indeed soar. Of course, you'll always have something that you'll want to change about yourself, because as long as you live and breathe you will remain a work in progress. But, you were created to live an extraordinary life, so enjoy the ride!

Idea File:

My Thoughts, Ideas and Plans of Action:

_____

_____

_____

_____

_____

_____

_____

_____

_____

_____

_____

_____

_____

_____

_____

_____

_____

_____

_____

_____

_____

_____

_____

_____

 # Idea File:

My Thoughts, Ideas and Plans of Action:

_____

_____

_____

_____

_____

_____

_____

_____

_____

_____

_____

_____

_____

_____

_____

_____

_____

_____

_____

_____

_____

_____

_____

**Idea File:**

My Thoughts, Ideas and Plans of Action:

_____

_____

_____

_____

_____

_____

_____

_____

_____

_____

_____

_____

_____

_____

_____

_____

_____

_____

_____

_____

_____

_____

# Idea File:

My Thoughts, Ideas and Plans of Action:

_____

_____

_____

_____

_____

_____

_____

_____

_____

_____

_____

_____

_____

_____

_____

_____

_____

_____

_____

_____

_____

_____

Notes

#1 Dare to Dream
1. Peter Daniels, *How to Reach Your Life's Goals: Keys to Help You Fulfill Your Dreams* (Honor Books, 1995)

#2 Write Your Life's Mission Statement.
1. Random House Webster's College Dictionary:
Tony Geiss/Published 1996

#3 Set Too Many Goals
1. Peter Daniels, *How to Reach Your Life's Goals: Keys to Help You Fulfill Your Dreams* (Honor Books, 1995)

#7 Communicate with Confidence
1. Taken from the Christian Business Man Magazine Sept/Oct 1998 (written by George Silver)

#12 Love Your Husband
1. Harvey & Marilyn Diamond, *Fit For Life* (Warner Books 1987)

All Scriptures taken from the Holy Bible
The King James Version (KJV)
New International Version (NIV)
New King James Version (NKJV)
or The Living Bible (TLB)

25 Ways Ordinary Women Can Live Extraordinary Lives **contains only suggestions concerning health and nutrition, before taking any action, please visit or counsel with your physician.**

About the Author

Stacia Pierce has a message of optimism that tells women there is greatness in them. Stacia focuses on the possibilities for women instead of the limitations. She illuminates purpose and direction in others and gives them the motivation to live above average.

A popular speaker who travels nationwide for seminars, workshops and conferences; Stacia carries out her mission to train, inspire and lead women to live truly successful lives. Due to her enthusiasm, charisma and ability to communicate with people of all ages, women are compelled to create a life worth living.

Stacia is the author of six books, thirteen leadership manuals, Editor-in-Chief of *W.O.R.D.* Magazine, director of a women's leadership team, on the advisory council of *Aspire* Magazine. founder of *Women in the Word*, as well as the Women's Success Institute and the host of the international Women's Success Conference.

She has a heart for women and anyone exposed to her ministry will have their lives changed forever.

Stacia, her husband Pastor James and their two children: Ryan and Ariana reside in Lansing, MI.

Audio Cassettes by Stacia Pierce

Below is a small sample of the awesome audio cassette teachings Stacia available. To order or to receive a complete listing, please call: 517-333-9860

THE SOCIAL SAVVY SERIES

The Social Savvy Series lessons are packed with power points, quick tips and handy information to equip you to be socially confident.

Item #	Title	Price
SS62	Disciplines of a Happy Home (5)	$25.00
SS63	How to Build Proper Friendships (2)	$10.00
SS64	How to Journalize (2)	$10.00
SS65	Tea Breaks w/ Stacia Pierce (1)	$5.00
SS67	A Woman's Personal Space (1)	$5.00
SS68	How to Celebrate the Seasons (1)	$5.00
SS69	The Art of Taking Care of You	$5.00

Women In The Word

This collection of tape series are great for personal and spiritual growth. Stacia covers topics important to women and provides matter-of-fact, insight to better living.

SS70	The Achievers Notebook	$5.00
W14	How To Build the Life You Want (2)	$10.00
W20	The Power of Positive Words (2)	$10.00
W21	How Prayer Can Change Your Life (1)	$5.00
W23	How to Walk in Divine Favor (1)	$5.00
W24	How to Have Enjoyment & Fulfillment in Your Marriage (1)	$5.00

THE *Women's* SUCCESS AUDIO CLUB

It's the audio magazine you've been waiting for! Get your subscription today. Each month Stacia shares a motivational message with practical solutions to life's challenges. With the Women's Audio Club you will gain a balanced comprehensive approach to creating your success.

C5	Frame Your Future (1)	$6.00
C6	Getting Great Ideas (1)	$6.00
C7	How to Look & Feel Like a Million (1)	$6.00
C10	Great Agendas for Good Success (1)	$6.00
C14	How to Live a Rewarding Life (1)	$6.00

WSI

The Women's Success Institute

STACIA PIERCE, FOUNDER

THE WOMEN'S SUCCESS INSTITUTE (WSI) IS DEDICATED TO TRAINING AND MENTORING CHRISTIAN WOMEN TO BE EQUIPPED TO FULFILL THEIR GOD-GIVEN TASK. WSI IS A PROGRAM OF LIFE CHANGERS CHRISTIAN CENTER, HEADED BY STACIA PIERCE AND WILL OFFER SPECIAL WORKSHOPS FOR WOMEN WHO ARE CHOOSING LEADERSHIP.

SESSIONS SUCH AS *HOW TO WRITE A BOOK, HOW TO PREPARE A MESSAGE, HOW TO BUILD A WOMEN'S LEADERSHIP TEAM* AND MUCH MORE WILL BE HELD EXCLUSIVELY FOR WSI MEMBERS ONLY. WSI WILL PROVIDE YOU WITH RE-SOURCES, EDUCATION, TRAINING AND CERTIFICATION TO HELP WOMEN SERVE GOD IN THEIR LOCAL CHURCH, MINIS-TRY OR PROFESSIONAL CAREERS.

YOU'LL RECEIVE:

A BIMONTHLY NEWSLETTER packed with ideas and information, for women who lead.

SPECIAL DISCOUNT RATES for selected WSI sponsored events and selected materials from Stacia Pierce

PRAYER SUPPORT of Stacia Pierce and the women's leadership team. As a member, you will be under their continual prayer covering

PRIORITY BOOKING with Stacia Pierce.

PARTNERSHIP NETWORKING during the annual Women's Suc-cess Conference and other WSI events, will create a strong net-work of support with other women leaders.

PARTNERSHIP WOMEN'S MINISTRY PACKET full of re-sources to equip you for leadership.

Women's Success Institute Application

Name: _____

Address: _____

City: _____ State _____ Zip _____

Phone: daytime # :(_____)_____ -_____

       evening #:(_____)_____

E-mail:_____ Fax: (_____)_____

Church Name:_____

Church Address: _____

City: _____ State _____ Zip _____

Ministry Position: _____

or Job Title (if applicable): _____

What do you need most from Stacia Pierce and the **WSI**? Explain:

_____

_____

_____

_____

_____

_____

What leadership roles are you already actively involved in?

_____

_____

_____

To become a lifetime member of the Women's Success Institute and receive my **WSI** Portfolio Packet loaded with informative "tip sheets." simply send **$49.95** along with this completed form to:

Life Changers Christian Center
808 Lake Lansing Road Ste. 200
East Lansing, MI 48823
517-333-9860

The Women's SUCCESS Audio Club
with STACIA PIERCE

MOTIVATIONAL TEACHING BY STACIA PIERCE, WITH PRACTICAL SOLUTIONS AND LIFE CHANGING INFORMATION. STACIA WILL CAUSE YOU TO EXPAND YOUR VISION, IMPROVE YOUR MINISTRY SKILLS AND INSPIRE YOU TO HAVE SUCCESS WITH GOD!

SPECIAL BONUS WOMEN'S BOOKCLUB NEWSLETTER: STACIA WILL KEEP YOU UP TO DATE AND INFORMED BY PROVIDING YOU WITH BOOKS AND RESOURCES THAT WILL CHANGE YOUR LIFE.

GET IDEAS THAT WILL CAUSE YOU TO EXCEL IN YOUR HOME, RELATIONSHIPS AND MINISTRY.

SIGN UP TODAY AND RECEIVE THE MOST AWESOME SUCCESS PRINCIPLES FOR DAILY LIVING THAT YOU'VE EVER HEARD.

TO ORDER YOUR 12 MONTH SUBSCRIPTION, SIMPLY COMPLETE THE INFORMATION BELOW, ENCLOSE **$69.95** AND SEND TO:

**LIFE CHANGERS CHRISTIAN CENTER
808 LAKE LANSING ROAD STE. 200
EAST LANSING, MI 48823
517-333-9860**

Name:_____

Address:_____

City:_____State:_____Zip:_____

Phone: Day ( )_____ Evening ( )_____

Payment Method: ❑cash ❑check ❑money order ❑credit card

❑Master Card ❑VISA ❑American Express ❑Discover

Card#:_____Exp. Date_____

Cardholder's signature_____

Other Books by Stacia Pierce

The Christian Women's Guide to Health and Nutrition

25 Ways Women Can Motivate Themselves

25 Ways Moms Can Raise Extraordinary Kids

The Success Secrets of a Reader

The Prayer & Purpose Planner

I'd love to hear from you. I invite you to share your thoughts and comments concerning this book. Please write me.

Fondly, Stacia

To receive more information about additional materials by Stacia Pierce, or engage her for Seminars, or Women's Conferences, please call or write:

Life Changers Christian Center
808 Lake Lansing Road Suite 200
East Lansing, MI 48823
517-333-9860